to Carmel 'X/1/03
from Karen
& Dr Darland
you are a very
good Woman!
So Nice to meet you

<u>BOOK</u>

<u>TRIM FOR LIFE</u>

By Harry Darland, M.D.

Consult your physician before starting any diet, exercise and medicine program. This is of particular importance if you are over 35 and have been inactive for a period of time. The author and publisher disclaim any liability from loss, injury or damage, personal or otherwise, resulting from the procedures and instructions in this book.

Forward

We now have a way... a way to lose weight for those who find it so hard to do.

This is an eclectic book that encompasses all means for optimal weight and fitness. Its emphasis is on <u>drugs</u> - now mainly Phentermine, Xenical, Meridia and Prozac "Phen-Xen" or "Phen-Xen-Pro". Of course proper diet considerations and exercise is a necessary corollary for this management toward a cure of Overweightness, along with of course Behavioral Modification (lifestyle changes) and maybe surgery. This entire pattern is based on the simple (and complicated) fact that Obesity-Overweightness is a genetic, physiological, psychological fact of life. It is not your fault. You didn't ask to be born with these circumstances, but you were; and these circumstances are real and causative. It stems back to the fact that self-preservation is our main need. Mother nature wants us to survive; so she evolved the hypothalamus in our brains that makes us hungry; and when were not hungry gives us an appetite for all sorts of foods. This is so we will pack on the weight to survive the famine – periods without food. We can live 4 minute without oxygen; 4 days without water; but as much as 4 months without any food at all – if we've packed it on (mainly the energy in stored fat). This is a survival mechanism. We have lived some 4 ½ - 5 million years as hominids, and some 200,000 years as homosapiens sapiens. Along came planting, herding, the polis, the society, the motorized wheel and in civilized societies ample food – especially high in fat. And voila, here is our dilemma. How do we get back to the active homosapiens, who ate much less food in general, especially fat? We work with our ancient mind, modern brains, and we manipulate our environment to the benefit of healthy minds, and bodies. That is how! That's what this book is about.

Overweightness has to be combated with all the tools we have available: proper diet, good exercise, good lifestyle, medicine, and, in some cases, possibly surgery. But, mostly this project is going to be accomplished by drugs under proper supervision for the whole program. This is the way. This is what our book Trim For Life is about.

I have no connection to anyone, except my patients and the truth. I have had this interest since I picked up my first barbell at age 14. I got my medical license as a physician and surgeon and have practiced total, general Family Medicine ever since. My experience in fitness and weight reduction techniques has brought me to this point in our practice of medicine for the treatment of this problem/disease. There are many more advances we have to make and many more techniques and medicine; but, we have come far enough to help millions of people. We must accept these four premises:

1. Overweightness is primarily a genetic problem; - probably 95%

2. Diet, especially fats, is very important;

3. Exercise and other lifestyle changes

are critical; and

4. Taking drugs, such as appetite suppressants and other pharmaceuticals, like the "Fat-Blocker" Xenical, is especially critical now and in the future; and sometimes doing surgery may be the answer.

We can do a lot toward the cure of Overweightness for millions right now. Let's all get on with it. The main question to me is will this book be a help or a hindrance? If it's the former, my project will have been helpful and gratifying to many, as well as to myself.

My Best and Sincerest Regards,

Harry W. Darland, M.D.
Family Physician, A.A.F.P.
Rockford, Illinois USA

An Expression of Appreciation - Thank You!

When an author takes on such a formidable project as broad and encompassing as weight loss, health, and fitness, they need all the help they can get. It is a feat; and I appreciate all the help I've had from my dear wife, Karen, my family, my associates and colleagues in my profession of Medicine, my patients, my dear friends, and my partners in the "work-out/running" scene.

I was fortunate to have been brought up in the "wilds" as a farm boy - to see and experience the effects of "Mother Nature." My experiences in the village of Oswego, Illinois, was further nurturing toward the ideas of fitness and health. I received a very good primary education; first in our one-room schoolhouse in Oskaloosa, Iowa, under our "school-marm", Hattie, then under "Miss Brooks" in Oswego. Our school system followed the basic principles of Thomas Jefferson (1743) and John Dewey (1859) in their philosophies of a broad-based education. Reading, Writing, and Arithmetic were emphasized, as were Music, Art and Sports. Health and Fitness were emphasized both mentally and physically. These were good years of training under the home tutelage of Mom, Dad, Grandma's, Grandpa's and helpful neighbors.

I was active in all sports: Football, Baseball, Track (Pole-vaulting); and I was fortunate to have two wonderful teachers of Music in Mr. James Trotto at East High School in Aurora, Illinois and Mrs. Margaret F. Pouk, of the Music Appreciation course in high school. She asked us, among other things, who we appreciated more as an opera tenor, Caruso, Mario Lanza, or the great Jussi Bjoring.

The YMCA was a very influential source and provided impressive information in "Hi-Y', our athletics and swimming. Our leaders there were directive and encouraging toward a field of work in "Y" principles, and hopefully (for me), to be a YMCA professional. The Korean War directed me further when I experienced the supreme fitness atmosphere of the 82nd Airborne paratroopers, with many good associations and instruction.

I finally decided on the field of medicine and did pre-med at Aurora College, Aurora, and North Central College, Naperville. After serving in the Army as a sergeant during war time and having one combat excursion to Lebanon under President Eisenhower (we did not drop, the marines did the job), I was ready for education, and I studied hard in college. Whereas I floundered in High School, I received 5 A's my first semester in college. I decided on Medicine then and was fortunate to go the prestigious University of Illinois College of Medicine in Chicago, with all of its affiliates like Rush-Presbyterian and Cook County Hospital. I am indebted to all of my wonderful College and University professors; one of who is still my mentor and, now my good friend, Dr. Gerald Hoffman, Psychiatrist, of Rockford, Illinois.

At Rockford Memorial Hospital, Rockford, Illinois, I took my internship under the great tutelage of teachers like Family Physician, Dr. John McHugh and Surgeon, Dr. William Boswell. After internship, I set up a General Practice. Winnie Ragan was my first patient. I thank her for her confidence. Since then I have had many patients trust in my judgement and skills in the Family Practice of Medicine, including Obstetrics. We have delivered over 3,000 babies now, and even some of their babies.

In all, my focus has been on Preventative Medicine, fitness and health. Much of this work has had to do with diet and exercise. I thank all those wonderful patients who have helped to guide me in helping them to optimal fitness and health. Many of them were weight-reduction patients who needed a physician's help. That is where our motivation started. I want to thank my patient, Chandra Johnson; later joined by others, who gave me the support to try using Phen-Fen. My further thanks go to the catalyst/jump that Dr. Michael Weintraub, Stephen Lamm, Sheldon Levine, and others gave in the idea that medicine and surgery may be a necessity in treating overweightness in the short, and long run.

I thank Dr. Richard Atkinson, President of the American Obesity Association and speaker at our hospital in December, 1995; inviting me to be a charter member of the American Obesity Association (A.O.A.) in 1996. I also thank the members and officers (some 5,000) of the American Society of Bariatric Physicians (ASBP) for inviting me to be a member in 1997.

I want to thank all of our children and their families for being so supportive and understanding in this endeavor. My seven brothers and sisters, and the rest of my lovely family.

I want to thank my three "author" friends, Rick Nielsen, Tom Heflin, and David Calderwood, and their families for the encouragement to stay "bold".

I want to thank my partners: Dr. Charles Inskeep, Dr. Charles Washington, and Dr. Bassam Soufan for putting up with my "trips", call arrangements, as well as their support.

I want to thank my staff- Linda Swisher, Laurel Ozburn, Cheryl Goecke, and their manager, again, my wife, Karen.

I want to thank Mollie Hughes and her husband Todd, Gate Pharmaceutical Representative, for all their good help with this general topic and the Adipex-P tablet, aids, and her encouragement to Karen and myself, as well as our patients over the last 10 years.

I want to thank my work-out buddies: Mike DeDoncker, Michael Smith, and Willie Graves for their "push" and camaraderie. My running friends will always be dear and in my mind: John Whitehouse, Bob Sewell, Henry Gallenz, Paul Johnson, and many, many others.

I want to thank Ernie Frantz, President of the World Powerlifting Federation. I met Ernie and his brother Victor when I instructed weight lifting at the YMCA in Aurora, Illinois in 1956. They asked me "can we join your weight lifting class, Mr. Darland?" I said "sure" and they have been my friends ever since.

I want to thank Georgene Daughtry and her family: husband, Kevin and son Joshua. She's my tireless transcriptionist, typist and "syntax" expert. You are very dear to me.

I want to thank Jim Ross, Chicago representative for the Worzalla Publishing Company of Stevens Point, Wisconsin, for all your help.

My patients, my staff and I would like to thank Edward Bruno, attorney, Chicago, Illinois; and former Prosecutor of the Illinois Department of Professional Regulations for his help in the legal aspects of prescribing anorexiant drugs for overweightness - obesity. Ed is an excellent endurance athelete as well as an exellent attorney.

I want to thank Michael Reiter, attorney, Chicago, Illinois and Jim Gotz, attorney, Boston, in their help to me in presenting data about Fenfluramine. Their help in this book is very much appreciated - in keeping it "scientific".

Karen and I would like to thank our family attorney William Howard, Rockford, Illinois, for all his help over the last 20 years. Including in the reading of this book and his advice in regards to this project over the last 6 years.

I want to thank Cheryl Goecke for getting the final typing ready for Kinko's.

I want to thank Kim Kistner, Branch Manager , and Tyler Gilmore, Project Manager, with the Kinko's branch in Rockford, Illinois; for typesetting this book in the "font" that I wanted, making the final print and for other helpful suggestions.

Lastly, thank you again, dear Karen; my lovely wife, wonderful friend and fellow worker in this important project - thank you for me, our patients and others; some of whom need this help so very much!

Modern Medicine's new cure for obesity is the key to weight control and better health for millions. We are entering a new age of unprecedented potential for healthier men, women, and children - with lower medical costs. In _Trim For Life: 21st Century Medicine And The New You_, Dr. Harry Darland explains clearly and fully what this medical breakthrough can mean for you and how you and your loved ones can reap its full benefits.

Notes:

Notes:

Chapter One

In this chapter, you will learn about my patients who are able to overcome chronic weight control problems with the modern, holistic approach I advocate. They are able to attain and maintain normal, fit, healthy weight and find new enjoyment in life - once and for all! And you will learn that the same help which has changed their lives is available to you in your doctor's office.

Patients' Personal Comments

"I've been on every diet possible the last 30 years of my life. Losing - gaining, trying another and losing - gaining. With other diets it takes you so long to lose 15 to 20 pounds that you start to get bored and go off it. With this you lost fast and even if you think about eating something bad, the thought comes back to you of the progress you are risking and you say 'I don't need it.

Helpless and Hopeless?
Not Any More.

Helpless and hopeless are words many of my patients have used to describe their feelings about being overweight. *But not anymore.*

As a family doctor committed to my patients' wellness and seeing first hand how much disease and suffering are directly related to being overweight, I felt the same way my patients did. But not anymore.

The first step toward solving any problem is recognizing the problem. If you have a weight control problem, recognizing it is easy.

You look in a mirror - and you know.

Clothes don't fit right - and you know.

A friend mentions that you're gaining weight - and you know.

You know when your mother or your mate says something like, "Honey, you really should be watching your weight." or your visit to the doctor ends with your doctor saying, "and I want you to start working on that weight, too. It's part of the problem."

Even children will tell you, as one of my six year old patients did when she was sitting next to Georgia, a young mother in my office waiting room. The six year old looked at Georgia, who was about 100% overweight - and innocently asked, "Why are you so fat?"

Georgia told the little six-year old, Carrie, "I can't help it, I was born this way."

She was right. Georgia actually was "born that way." And she actually couldn't help it then. But not anymore.

I know, because Georgia was the first baby I delivered at the beginning of my family practice more than three decades ago and has been a lifelong patient. Georgia is now a high-level management executive, besides being a mother, and I have delivered her babies. Through the years, she - I should say we - have tried every available approach to attain and maintain her normal, healthy weight level. Despite our efforts year in and year out, weight control continued to be a problem. *But not anymore.*

Now she is on a program which combines the common sense approaches of diet and exercise which we have always known with carefully prescribed and monitored medication developed in breakthrough research by medical science. For the first time in her - and our - many attempts, she is making it!

This development is as exciting and gratifying for me as it is for my patients because now, for the first time in my 30 years of practice as a family doctor with this an area of major emphasis, I am able to cure obesity, to help intractably overweight patients attain and maintain healthy, fit, and normal weight.

My goal in this book is to share that experience with you and explain how you can have the same life-changing, life-enhancing, life-saving benefits in you life - after you have learned that you can do it and have decided that you want to do it.

"Why are you fat?" was the straightforward, innocent though insensitive question the little six-year-old asked Georgia in my office. My physical training experience, my medical education, and my years of experience as a General Practitioner now compel me to conclude that if you knew the answer to that question, you would not be overweight. You would be normal weight, fit, and even more attractive and self-assured.

If you are like many of my patients, you have had the support and encouragement, in addition to the wisdom and expertise, of the traditional helpers in you struggle with weight control: psychologists, psychiatrists, nutritionists, trainers, and sympathetic, compassionate friends. And you have found them helpful, but not completely successful. You have been left with repeated failures despite repeated attempts because you have been missing an essential element: the carefully prescribed and monitored medication and, in some cases, surgery now available through doctors whose focus is preventing disease and fostering wellness rather than merely treating illness.

I said before that my primary goal in this book is to share my experience with you and to explain how you also can have the same life-changing, life-enhancing, life-saving benefits in your life. I have another goal, perhaps equally important because of the ramifications for health care. My second goal is to encourage doctors everywhere to become informed and begin dealing with this critical problem, which afflicts and kills so many. It is not enough for us to know and understand the problem. We must know, understand, and use the safe and effective means now available to cure obesity and sustain lifelong fitness. George Blackburn, Harvard University Nutrition Center, our esteemed leader in this field - our "guru".said at a recent meeting this year in Greensboro, N.C., "only 10% of primary doctors are proactive in the treatment of obesity-overweightness". This is a critical issue. We all have to get involved in everyway we can.

Tell your doctor about the approaches to your weight problem I am going to share with you from my own research and clinical experience. Tell him or her about the new medicine or surgical approaches, the research of others, including Knoll and Roche Laboratories and individuals like Blackburn, Arrone, Franke, Bray, Lucas, Lamm, Levine. And like Dr. Richard Atkinson, described in the next chapter. Doctors everywhere need to learn that applying the full power of medical science to the elimination of obesity is not the work of renegades, but of trailblazers on the frontier of wellness through weight control, exercise, good nutrition, medicine, and surgery. As you will discover in the following pages, we need all the help we can get to spread the word!

Notes:

_____

_____

_____

_____

_____

_____

_____

_____

_____

_____

_____

_____

_____

_____

_____

_____

_____

_____

_____

_____

_____

_____

_____

_____

Notes:

_____

_____

_____

_____

_____

_____

_____

_____

_____

_____

_____

_____

_____

_____

_____

_____

_____

_____

_____

_____

_____

_____

_____

_____

_____

Patient's Personal Comments

"Food no longer controls me! I can go to the grocery store and buy only what's on my list! I can go to social events and never lay eyes on the food table. Even my favorite foods I am able to pass up. It's a great feeling!"

"I have only been heavy 10 years. The heavier I would get the lower the self-esteem, the more I ate. Now I know there's hope; I'll be my old self again. Watch out world, I'm back!

<u>Chapter Two</u>

In this chapter, you learn the essentials in weight loss are diet, exercise, lifestyle changes, medicine and surgery, but mostly for the many who find weightloss stubborn - the medicine.

Patient's Personal Comments

"The medicines really do help,I use to crave and devour high fat, high salt, high sugar snacks. I could never skip a meal or snacks - I was starving! I can really tell the difference in cravings for before and after meal snacks and a large rich dinner.

You Need Medicine - And Why You Need Medicine

Forty percent of adults in the USA - 36% of men and 40% of women - are now seriously overweight, enough to be unhealthy, according to the National Health and Nutrition Examination Survey just completed. There are more then 50 percent overweight by 20 percent.

What is worse, the number of seriously overweight men and women, those overweight by 20% or more, is increasing rapidly - up 25% since 1980. A recent newspaper report in USA Today said that 54% of America is overweight and that number is growing at 1% per year!

Even children are falling victim to the health risks and social stigma of being overweight at a faster rate than their overweight parents: 14% of those ages 6 to 19 are overweight today, compared with just 8% in 1980, and 12% of adolescents age 12 to 17, double the 6% in 1980, and many of them are getting diabetes.

The needless loss of life related to such excess weight is staggering. Each year there are at least 300,000 preventable deaths definitely attributable to being overweight and it's growing.

The diminished quality of life and the cost ramifications for health care are equally staggering: obesity plays a major role in a myriad of minor and major illnesses, including heart disease, diabetes, and hypertension.

Why should this be happening? What are we in the medical community doing about it? What can we do about it?

Many doctors in the past - and, yes, some even now - would tell a patient, "You're overweight. Its bad for you. Go on a diet and lose weight." And then - Viola! - the patient would go home and go on a diet and lose weight, yes? NO! Of course not!

Why not?

Some answers are found in the research on the causes and treatment of obesity by Dr. Richard Atkinson, president of the newly formed American Obesity Association. In his work with 2,500 patients at his University of Wisconsin at Madison clinic and his studies of past research and present knowledge of obesity and its treatment; Dr. Atkinson has found that obesity often is a physiological medical disease, which requires medicines to treat and cure. Dr. Atkinson and his research were cited by U.S. News & World Report in a 1995 analysis of approaches to dealing with obesity titled, "When Willpower Won't" - how apt and true!

Failure to maintain proper weight is the underlying cause of so much illness and suffering and so many persons are unable to control their weight without medical assistance. Medicine and surgery provide hope and help for relief from both the emotional distress of obesity and the many physical diseases which stem from it. Unfortunately, the scientific approach threatens the financial security of those with a vested interest in overweight, unhealthy people - which has now grown into a $50 billion a year industry - these are the people that medicine and surgery can cure of their weight control problems with a scientific approach.

As with any medical breakthrough, especially one which has great potential for reducing profits in large segments of the nation's so-called "health care" industry, legitimate medicine and surgery have now become controversial. Legitimate expressions of safety concerns about any medication are normal, beneficial, and helpful. They assist the Food and Drug Administration in its careful review process and protect us from harm. However, attacks by those for whom sick Americans are a gold mine, those who profit from illness and disease, are neither beneficial nor helpful. Even though the Food and Drug Administration had approved Phentermine, Meridia, and Xenical, and despite positive research findings and clinical experience cited here and elsewhere, attacks continue and cause medicine and surgery to be widely misunderstood and maligned.

It is imperative that medicines be

carefully prescribed and used with proper monitoring by your doctor. That is a given. All medications must be carefully prescribed and used with proper monitoring. And all medications, including Phentermine and Xenical and Fluoxetine (Prozac), must be administered with due consideration for any possible risks or side effects. When risks or side effects are exaggerated, however, wisdom compels us to consider the sources of the exaggerations and examine their motivation, especially when loss of large profits is involved. More on this aspect of the medical approach to weight control will be presented in later chapters.

My interest and approach in the medical treatment of obesity and overweightness increased when I read the 1990-1992 research papers written by Dr. Michael Weintraub of Rochester, New York. Dr. Weintraub is the physician who first discovered the efficacy of combining Phentermine and Fenfluramine and presented the first convincing evidence in favor of the Phen-Fen approach. One research report

I found to be particularly interesting and important was a long term, doubleblind, randomized, placebo-controlled study of 506 overweight females and 56 overweight males. It showed a 30% greater weight reduction in patients who followed the Phen-Fen approach and received the real medication than there was in those who did everything the same but were given a Phen-Fen substitute - a placebo in this approach

As my own interest was growing, patients also began bringing me articles and urging me to look more deeply into Phen-Fen. So I did. In addition to the U.S. News & World Report article cited above, a particularly good article also appeared in Reader's Digest.

I read *Thinner At Last*, a book written by Dr. Steven Lamm, who is a primary care doctor like me. Dr. Lamm is a brilliant A.O.A.(Alpha Omega Alpha) Scholastic Honorary Society doctor who saw the great need and practical use for the two medications which Dr. Weintraub had put together so successfully.

Dr. Lamm, like Dr. Weintraub, recognized that most diet, exercise, and behavior modification plans have not worked in a sustained way for half of American adults and one fifth of American children. Both recognized that we have tried a wide array of programs and approaches with various emphases and combinations, but those programs and approaches do not work for great numbers of overweight men, women, and children.

Those factors, their own research, and data gathered through clinical experience led both Dr. Lamm and Dr. Weintraub to conclude that, for many, obesity is a pathology, a disease, that is not the patients' fault, though they have been "blamed" for it as though it were their fault. And both concluded that, as a disease, which is part medical-physiological and part medical-psychological; it requires use of proactive medicines, which address both components for full and adequate treatment. Even though the Phen-Fen combination is discontinued for further research or use, they started the ball rolling.

Old, time-worn programs and approaches have not worked for so many because they have failed to treat the medical dimensions of the problem and because they have tried to treat all weight control problems as though there were only one cause. In fact, as many Bariatricians - whose specialty is treating obesity - and other medical doctors have observed recently, there are innumerable types and causes of obesity.

There are the imposingly overweight people who have been that way since childhood. When you look at family photos, they are the unfortunate people who stand out because of their excess body weight. They are the people with the so-called obesity gene.

Many others begin to struggle with obesity after childhood. They fit into the group Dr. Louis Aronne, Associate Professor of Medicine at Cornell University, Ithaca, New York, describes as patients who have "environmental triggers" such as trauma, often to the head, or severe psychological trauma such as an assault. Other environmental triggers include pregnancy, depression, separation, and losses. Dr. Aronne also has pointed out that some obesity, like hypertension and adult onset diabetes, may come on at a certain time of life when the genes and physiology are somehow triggered.

Because causes of weight control problems are many and varied, you and your doctor must decide what is best for you in your specific situation. For some doctors, playing a greater role in fostering wellness through weight control may be new. You may even have to do as my patients did and bring this to your doctor's attention.

Do not be surprised if you meet indifference. You may even meet skepticism and resistance. The history of medicine is replete with both. Skepticism and resistance greeted developments such as Insulin which now saves the lives of diabetics, Penicillin which now saves the lives of persons threatened by infection, and even our standard dietary approaches which now assure that we receive sufficient vitamins and minerals to defeat diseases of dietary deficiency. Today we take those developments for granted.

It is important, however, for us to remember that healthy skepticism and caution also prevent mistakes and save lives. Information and knowledge are what overcame skepticism and resistance for Dr. Frederick Banting and Charles Best with Insulin, Dr. Alexander Fleming with Penicillin, and Dr. Joseph Goldberger with vitamins and nutrition. Information and knowledge to address any skepticism you may meet and to help you and your doctor consider a medical or surgical approach to your weight problem is the subject of our next chapter.

I personally feel that over 95% of overweightness is genetically caused - psychologically and physiologically genetic. This is a premise that has to be acknowledged or we won't make a dent in this stubborn, growing national problem of overweightness and obesity.

Patients Personal Comments

"The medication changes your focus. You are not so wrapped up in dieting. You are truly not hungry. You can concentrate on other things in your life. My stress level has decreased remarkably since being on the medication. I now take things one day at a time and I can do so more efficiently. "

"I have been 40 pounds overweight for eight years now. I'm happily married with two great kids. And although I've blamed giving up smoking for my weight, the truth is I just love food! It's been a hobby. I eat just because it tastes good - and what else is there to do while watching T. V. ? I've tried Slim Fast and diet pills, etc.; nothing helped I was either weak and shaky from hunger or I was bouncing off walls with an enormous heart rate. I saw a friend of mine go from a size 18 to size 7 in a matter of months. She referred me to Dr. Darland. The medication he prescribed is wonderful. I have no side effects and I don't

even want to eat all day. I feel more energetic and motivated Instead of four pieces of pizza, one satisfies me fine and instead of a cupcake, a walk or bike ride suits me. I actually like to exercise and watch my caloric intake now. "

Notes:

Notes:

Chapter Three

In this chapter, you will learn about the development of medicines associated with weight control and you will receive data to help you cut through misinformation and confusion about the medications. You will learn how they differ and which medications are both safe and effective.

Patients Personal Comments

"In the past I had tried many 'diet pills', from prescribed medicines to 'over-the-counter' and herbs. Dr. Darland's program has done the most for me without the 'up and downs' of other medicines.

Overcoming Fear By Knowing How It Works: A Little History

Fear is a powerful weapon, and diet medicine opponents use it well. The remedies for fear are knowledge, information, and understanding. In this chapter, I will provide you with all three.

It is important not to confuse fear with caution. I advocate caution because caution is clear thinking and clear thinking can save lives. Caution appeals to your intelligence. Fear plays upon your emotions. Caution is rational. Fear is not.

Because caution is a trait of intelligent people, camouflaging fear to look like caution is a favorite tactic of those who seek to manipulate the public. They use it to stampede even intelligent people in the wrong direction.

Diet medicine opponents foster fear with half-truths and distortions.

Those half-truths and distortions are what caused the tragic, paralyzing fear I recently observed in an overweight, hypertensive patient who dismissed without consideration the medicine program even though it could save his life. It is very likely that he will clog or hemorrhage one of his atherosclerotic, obstructed arteries and become one of the numbers on the chart of preventable death statistics I cited earlier - as do 55% of all Americans who die from atherosclerosis every year. The deadly half-truths and distortions stem from the bad reputations of the amphetamines - "speed," the "diet pill," the "street drug." Because his mind was filled with terrifying visions of such "mind altering stuff," the patient could not calmly and rationally consider the medical approach to weight control and its life-saving, life-enriching potential for him.

Not all overweight people require medical assistance to lose and maintain weight. Some can do it with diet, exercise, and behavior modification alone. However, the experience of so many who have repeatedly tried and failed and the swelling flood of weight-loss literature and programs tells us that it is very, very difficult to lose weight and perhaps even more difficult to maintain normal weight with diet, exercise, and behavior modification alone.

The medicine program, on the contrary, works in the majority of cases. It is safe and will be available to you at your primary care doctor's office - if he or she will learn about and establish the program, determine whether you are qualified for it, put you on it, and maintain your sustaining program.

The following information about the history of medications used for weight control and the exact description of how I had used anorexiants, appetite suppressants, and the fat blocker, Xenical, to help patients in my practice will provide you and your doctor with knowledge and understanding you may use to both exercise caution and rationally confront the fears fostered by medicine treatment opponents.

In 1927 Benzedrine was produced in the test tube. It was found to cut the appetite as well as shrink the nasal mucous membranes. Ten years later, Dexedrine was discovered. Enterprising marketers quickly developed its appetite suppressing qualities into a multitude of "diet pills" which eventually were found to have more unpleasant side effects than beneficial hunger suppressant effects. Some of those side effects were addiction and death from cardiac arrythmia.

Dexedrine is what gave rise to the "speed-freak" addicts. Eventually Dexedrine and its analogs became controlled drugs, which may be prescribed only by doctors with a special license and DEA number. The tightly monitored prescriptions may have to be written on triplicate forms and are highly scrutinized. Dexedrine is still very useful medication for treating Pickwickianism, Narcolepsy, and Attention Deficit Disorder. It also has other special applications. Currently, some that used to require "triplicate" don't, like Adderol and Dexedrine for ADD and ADHD (Attention Deficit and Hyperactivity Disorder) children and adults.

In 1957, the adrenergic medication Phentermine was discovered. Adrenergic medicine prevents the uptake or increases the secretion of Adrenaline such as epinephrine and norepinephrine in the brain. It comes in the form of "Ionamine," "Fasten," "Adipex-P," "OB tabs," and the generic Phentermine itself. Some of these drugs too, are not available as brands since the "Phen-Fen" debacle.

Properly used and monitored by your doctor, Phentermine is a safe medication, non-addictive and long-acting, with easy dose adjustability. Phentermine raises the energy level about a 1+ stimulation versus the 4+ stimulation of Dexedrine. Phentermine's medical-physiological effect is to cut the hunger; mainly, it allegedly increases the metabolism and generally leaves you feeling well. It can be a long-acting pill that stays in the system for about 12 hours. One of the precautions is that it should not be taken later than 12 hours before the patient goes to bed. Moreover, it is not addictive according to all published criteria and the extensive clinical studies by Drs. Weintraub, Atkinson, Lamm, cited earlier and by Dr. George Bray, past executive director of the Pennington Biomedical Research Center at Louisiana State University, and others.

About the same time that Phentermine was discovered, an anti-depressant called Fenfluramine, brand name Pondimin, was developed. I have been familiar with it and had prescribed it for my patients over the years in addition to prescribing other anti-depressants, which have favorably impressed me.

Fenfluramine is the sister Serotonin medication which Dr. Weintraub found augments the weight reduction effectiveness of Phentermine. It is a serotonin increaser and a Serotonin Selective Re-uptake Inhibitor, in similar pathways as Prozac, Zoloft, Celexa, Serzone, Effexor, Wellbutrin, Luvox, and Paxil, the most frequently prescribed anti-depressive medications in the world. Its physiological-psychological effect is to stabilize or increase the Serotonin and thereby diminish overeating cravings and bingeing which often are related to emotional states. The Serotonin drugs, in my opinion, are very safe medications when used properly.

I start my patients on the program with an essential history and physical; an orientation in diet focusing on low fat intake; counseling on an exercise program appropriate for their starting condition, and introduction of other lifestyle initiatives.

I use the history and physical to determine whether patients are medically eligible to participate in the program by making certain there are no pre-existing medical conditions, which would disqualify them. If a medically qualified patient happens to be more than 40% overweight, weighing 170 pounds when he or she should weigh 120, for example, then I begin the medication assistance prescription with one 30 milligram Phentermine tablet taken in the morning and one 120 milligram tablet of Xenical (the fat blocker) taken at each mealtime. The medication can be adjusted according to each patient's needs and in accordance with prescribing information allowances. Sometimes we used a serotonin drug like Prozac or others.

My patients leave the office with a packet on Adipex and Xenical, and if we use Prozac, an instruction sheet on that product is also sent. This packet includes a complete explanation of how the program works, customary medical information and precautions about medication reactions, the diet and behavior modification instructions, an exercise kit, and a diet diary. Like Dr. Lamm, I like my patients to write down what they eat and drink for one or two weeks out of the month, if their time and disposition will allow, to assure that they follow the absolutely essential adherence to the prescribed caloric restrictions. The medication can enhance the effect of the restricted calorie intake and make it easier for patients to live with the calorie restrictions by cutting down hunger and curbing food cravings, but the medication does not work without patients' dietary compliance. The medicine greatly helps that compliance, and with the fat blocker Xenical, 1/3 of the fat calories don't get in.

Taking Xenical does three things: it stops absorption of 1/3 of the fat you eat; it prevents your body from eating too much fat, or else it will cause diarrhea, cramps, or possibly slimy, sprayed flatulence. You know when you take the pill that it's to keep you on the diet; and it's costing good money, which is another motivator.

I see the patients in one month, by which time they often will have had a weight loss of 12 to 15 pounds. The second month we continue the program and try to lose an additional 10 to 12 pounds. On each subsequent visit we set goals for whatever seems best to us. I rarely go more than one to two pounds per week for those patients who are less than 20% from goal.

We try to reach goal weight in the third or fourth month. In some cases, it takes as long as a year. For the average patients I see in my family practice, I introduce a weight maintenance schedule from that point on, seeing the patients in one month, then again in two months, then every three to six months in the first year or two, depending on the patients' specific needs. If patients gain more than 5-8 pounds between their visits, it is an emergency. Their obesity-overweightness is "out of whack" and they come back immediately. In my opinion for most patients, after two years they've got it made. They are "cured." Their mind and body are recalibrated. There is new evidence that the brain may "reset" the "Hungerstat" and "appistat" with this program.

I never give patients more than a one-month supply of medication at any visit, even if they are stretching their medicine in the quarterly visits. For weight relapse or "pulsing," as Dr. Lamm calls it, we start right back at square one, if necessary, until we successfully attain and maintain the normal, healthy weight level for lifelong fitness. There are a significant number of "Re-Start" patients. They are hardly ever at the high weight they started with. The nature of the problem is chronic persistent fighting to stay at an optimal weight and to be fit and trim for life.

The weight-management patient is part of the usual busy day in which I am seeing patients from dawn to dusk. I may see an obstetric patient, a newborn, a heart patient, then my diet patient. They are integrated into the entire family practice. My wife Karen, my manager and medical assistant, and my nurse help me too; seeing patients on their own with my on-site supervision after the second visit.

The cost for the program is the office-call charge plus the medication the patient gets at the drug store. I allow flexibility in adjusting the dose and schedule. The patients may choose the popular Adipex-P brand Phentermine tablet, which is scored so you can break it in half if necessary and is titratable or adjustable, and the Meridia, Xenical, and any other medicines like Prozac. Whichever form they choose, the medical cost is less than many persons spend on cigarettes or alcohol and less than the cost of the food they would be eating without the medical assistance. The program becomes even more affordable if the savings in obesity related medical costs, lost income, and other financial, physical, and mental costs are included.

In my clinical experience, and in the research and studies cited, the medicine and this approach have been found safe and effective. I have used Phentermine, the hunger suppressing adrenergic; the serotonin drug, Prozac, and the fat blocker, Xenical, safely with younger patients as well as older patients and have found that, even for some hypertensives, cardiac, or psychiatric patients, the medicines especially Diethylproprion (Tentuate) can be titered or adjusted to the patients' needs with the approval and help of the specialist involved if necessary. Only 1% of Xenical is absorbed, so that only patients with gastrointestinal disturbances may have to be excluded.

It works. I see it in my bright-faced, exuberant, grateful, healthy, normal-weight patients! It is as wonderful and as life-saving as the other medical breakthroughs I mentioned earlier, though more subtle and slower-like the disease it cures.

It is those wonderful, life-saving results which have fueled my determination to write this book and counter the anti-medicine fears fostered by those with the questionable motives I cited earlier and will examine in greater depth later. This is after seeing some tens of thousands of patients from 1965, when I began the general practice of medicine, until now.

You may understand my enthusiasm more easily if you contrast what I am able to do for my patients now with what happened to me at a national weight control conference 25 years ago.

One of my patients, who was on the board of the national "Take Off Pounds Sensibly" (T.O.P.S.) organization, knew I had a special interest in helping overweight patients in my practice and that I had patients on diet programs. She was one of my monitored without medicine overweight patients in adjunct with the T.O.P.S. program.

About twenty-five years ago she asked me if I would speak to the National T.O.P.S. Annual Meeting taking place in the Midwest that year. It was to take place at our beautiful newly referbished Coronado Theater in Rockford, Illinois, where Bob Hope played Vaudeville in the 1930's. She wanted the topic to be titled, "How The Physician Treats Overweightness." I agreed and took about a month to prepare the speech, expecting to address a relatively small group of members, a few hundred at most.

As I came in the stage door and walked onto the stage for my introduction, all the house lights went out and the spotlight went on me. During the introduction, my eyes adjusted to the dark - and I was shocked as I looked out into the faces of about 3,000 eager, overweight people! They were all counting on me to show them the way.

I tried hard, delivering a carefully prepared speech with all the skill I could muster from my college training and speaking experience, but I went away with a feeling of sorrow that I did not have more help to offer those diligent, determined T.O.P.S. members.

That sorrow is gone now and I have the exact opposite feeling in my daily practice as a family doctor helping my overweight patients. Now I can apply the full power of medicine to cure obesity once and for all.

Knowledge, information, and understanding are necessary to use this new power properly and safely. But this new power is not the only area requiring us to have greater knowledge, information and understanding. Even in the basic areas of diet and nutrition, we have been sorely lacking. That is the topic of our next chapter.

Patients Personal Comments

"I was worried about the medicine and how it would effect my hypoglycemia. I was assured by Dr. Darland that I wouldn't have any problems. If I felt the 'attack' coming, he said to chew a piece of sugar gum. I had one 'attack'. I got the gum out - it did the trick. The medications have been easy to follow, even with my busy schedule. I purchased a cheap pillbox to keep some of the tablets in for those unexpected trips and overtime working hours. My attitude has done a 180-degree turn. I feel great. I have self-esteem again."

Notes:

Notes:

Chapter Four

    In this chapter, you will find valuable diet guidelines and answers to basic diet questions. It is my contention that there already is a glut of diet books available and I do not want to burden you with still more servings of diet information and recipes which you can easily get elsewhere. Of course, an essential element in successful weight control is calorie restriction, but you know that. It is not knowing what to do that is the problem. Applying it, getting there, and staying there, that is the hard part. My goal in this book is to make it easier for you to get there and stay there.

Patients Personal Comments

"After trying all sorts of diets for my moderate overweight state, nothing worked As the years came and went, pounds were added almost unnoticeably until the day I looked in the mirror then stood on the scale - and said, 'It's time to get serious!' Dr. Darland has helped me understand the weight process and I'm now feeling like I've got control in my life again. The medicine program works, as I've only been on it for three or four months and lost 18 pounds and have 12 more to go to my goal weight. It's all in the management and control of what we eat."

What Is The Best Diet?
What Should Homo Sapiens
(Wise Men) Eat?

Some argue that most doctors know little and care less about nutrition.

That is not a fair characterization, though it is easy to understand how the notion became popular when we consider how limited our medical school nutrition training was in the past. I can summarize what most of us were taught at our medical school lecture class in just a few words:

"Everyone should eat a well-balanced diet low in fat, including all of the main food groups the cereal-grain group, the vegetable-fruit group, the meat group, and the dairy group - in specified servings. A vitamin and mineral supplement is okay a few times a week or even every day. To maintain normal weight, the diet should balance energy input with energy output. In other words, the calories consumed in eating and drinking should match the calories burned in activities. To mobilize stored fat and lose weight, total calories taken in should be much less than total calories burned. Exercise is an important corollary to the diet regimen prescribed, and thinking pleasant thoughts is good for your eating, too."

There it is - everything we were taught. It is only fair and reasonable to note that this is essentially all we know with absolute and empirically supported certainty even today. That is why there is so much conjecturing, experimenting, and pure quackery in the nutrition field with annual costs to consumers in the billions of dollars.

Every day in my practice I deal with nutrition, as do all of my Primary Care Doctor colleagues. I have supplemented my training with thirty-five years of reading every cogent piece on nutrition that I could get my hands on, managing menus with the help of a college trained and certified nutritionist for a nursing home which I served as a director for 17 years, and writing every hospital patient dietary order for all of my patients, from those afflicted with major illnesses to those with relatively minor afflictions, from those just born to those aged or dying, and for everyone and everything in between.

Those and other experiences have heightened my awareness of the vital role nutrition plays in health and healing and have increased my conviction that American medical training must focus greater attention on the very important area of nutrition and the health of the body. We are improving, but we still devote the bulk of our time, effort, and study to treating diseases while sometimes ignoring or even demeaning all but the most elementary aspects of nutrition.

Many physicians remain ill-equipped in the area of medically applied nutrition beyond the most rudimentary level, insufficiently prepared to apply it in cases where it does not appear to be the central issue, and woefully unprepared to apply it in obesity treatment where it is the central issue. Knowing that obesity causes 300,000 preventable deaths in this country each year should provide us with the drive to increase our research and expand our knowledge. Saving lives, after all, is our main job.

One of our obstacles may be our medical mindset, the very way we think. As doctors, we are scientists accepting and operating on the scientific method. We are taught to observe, study, and prove. We gather facts, hypothesize, experiment, and draw conclusions. It is this training and natural inclination of physicians which make us effective in applying the cures available to us and saving lives as we do.

This does not mean we ignore the anecdotal information, which comes to us in reports of worthy medical results in individual patients. Nor do we fail to recognize something we might call style or art in healing, the quality which enables some physicians to have much better results with their patients even though they work with the same basic knowledge as physicians who are less successful.

Using the benefits of science, we apply the scientific approach of cause and effect to diagnose and treat our patients. And when all goes according to the standard hypothesis, our patients get well. Yet that has not been the case with obesity treatment and, until now, science has seemed to be stumped.

It has not been and is not now enough for us to tell our patients who are digging graves with forks, "Go on an diet and lose weight." Hypothetically, they will diet and lose weight. In reality, they do not. We must be prepared to direct them to and guide them through proper and healthy diet practices as part of our medical care. And when that guidance proves insufficient, we must be able to provide the medical-physiological as well as the medical-psychological assistance which produce the successful treatment results we have come to expect.

Diet guidance fosters wellness. Dr. Atkinson and every other Bariatrician, every researcher in the field of obesity, and every Primary Care Doctor emphasize that a critical and essential element in successful treatment of overweight patients is caloric restriction.

Dr. Atkinson reminds us that some of our dieting assumptions have proven false: that not all calories are equal; that some person may "eat like a bird" and still not be able to lose weight; that obesity is not a simple affliction with a single cause, but a complex condition with a host of causes; that despite what your mother may say, you don't have to eat breakfast or follow many of the other rigid rules once thought indispensable.

My diet directives to my patients call for well-balanced, divided meals, at least two rather than one continuous supper, with all of the food groups and, in some cases, vitamin and mineral supplements. I like the 1000-calorie a day approach to dieting for my patients with some adjustments in the few cases where they are warranted. I stress that one fat gram provides nine calories versus four to five calories for carbohydrates and protein and, therefore, like to stick to 30-40 fat grams per day if possible. I give my patients a pocket book size calorie counting book which has calories per food in the back index as well as a little "fat counting" book. They are very useful in helping patients stick to the obligatory and compulsory diet requirements.

Dr. Lamm recommends 1200 calories per day approach and Dr. Atkinson has said for very overweight patients the doctor may have to prescribe 400 to 800 calories only per day.

That's it for diet; finis, kaput, done. The real trick for many, of course, is not just knowing about diet. Some overweight people have libraries of diet books and probably could write a book about dieting themselves. It is not knowing what to do that is the problem; applying it, getting there, and staying there, that is the hard part.

I am ending this chapter on diet with the following 10 basic tips based on a calorie counting book I give my patients

1. The little things are often your undoing. Two cups of coffee, each with two lumps of sugar and two tablespoons of cream, add up to 130 calories. Two cups with no-calorie sweetener and non-dairy cream provide only

22 calories - more than a five-fold difference. Be alert for highcount, sneaky calories you can easily avoid.

2. With every decade past your 13th birthday, calorie requirements drop by about 10 percent. If at 40 you're eating exactly as you were at 20, don't be surprised by the bulges. Unless you're exceptionally active, you'll have to cut back as you get older to stay even. This effect is easily observable and probably is true because most of us tend to have less exercise as we age.

3. It's always a battle between the goops and the crisps. All the lovely gooey things - butter, cream, mayonnaise, salad oil, ice cream, gravies, mousses - have calorie multipliers in the hundreds, while - celery radishes, cucumbers, lettuce, dill pickles - are low in calories you can eat almost unlimited amounts and never notice. In fact, if you reject the goops in favor of the crisps, you may not have to do any other dieting - if you stick to the "balance" equation, matching calories consumed with

calories burned.

4. If a person in your life is struggling with weight control, you can help him or her by not only substituting an apple for the apple pie dripping with ice cream, but also explaining why. Many people, even those who are highly educated, simply don't understand the basics about food. "I just had a hamburger for lunch," they may say, neglecting to mention that they also consumed a pile of French fries, several fried onion rings and a large hamburger roll smothered with catsup - something over 1,000 calories in all.

5. Beware of the so-called diet fruit platters in many restaurants. The cantaloupe balls have about 30 calories and the grapefruit sections another 30, but the canned pear half can weigh in at 78, the canned peach at 90, the fruit gelatin at 80, the cottage cheese at 50 and the dressing, which you probably pour on generously since you're feeling so virtuous, at least 80. This is a total of 438 calories. The fruit is good for you, but don't be fooled into

thinking you've hardly had a calorie.

6. As fat melts away, your body often fills with water - especially if you're a woman in the middle years or older. Water accumulation explains why you can be faithful to your diet and see no weight loss reflected on your scales. A good way to reduce water retention is to cut down on salt and increase your physical activity. No diuretics, please, unless your doctor specifically orders them - though this aspect varies a great deal.

7. Don't fast for more than two or three days without strict medical supervision. A 24- or 48-hour abstention from solid food (while drinking water, juice or other low- or no-calorie fluids) can leave you tingling with triumph and several pounds lighter - for a few days anyway. But long-term fasting without protein supplements and careful monitoring of vital functions may be harmful to muscle and vital organ tissue, although many of us could go for four weeks or even 4 months without eating and stay alive.

8. When it comes to gaining or losing weight, your body may or may not distinguish between 400 calories in a pork sausage and the same number of calories in a chunk of chocolate cake. The calories you do avoid, however, should always be the most expendable - those which contain the least protein, vitamins, and minerals. Fifty calories are very well invested in a glass of orange juice, poorly spent on a sugary soft drink.

9. While a lot is known about the relationship between calories and body weight, even the most diligent researchers still can't explain why some people seem to defy the rules. We've all met the pencil-slim person who packs away malted milks, martinis and whipped cream-crowned Irish coffees on top of seven-course dinners and never gains an ounce. We've also met the perennial chubby who puts on a couple pounds just from reading recipes (or so they claim). While theories about "glands" are given little credence by today's medical authorities, certain individuals do, it seems, have an unusual metabolic system that

requires huge amounts of food to carry on a normal days work. Instead of envying those eat-a-lots, just think of them as inefficient machines - too bad they have to stoke up on so much of that expensive fuel from the supermarket.

10. when you cross off cakes, pies, whipping cream, fat-larded steaks and roasts, fruit canned in heavy syrup and fatty foods of all kinds from your shopping list, your food budget goes a lot further in terms of nutrition. And when you cut costly meat and fish down to modest 100- or 200- calories servings, you'll find a roast, meatloaf, or a striped bass will provide twice as many meals as before. In other words, it really pays to count calories.

Enough about diet! If dieting alone were sufficient to solve the weight control problems we face, there would be far fewer books about it and more healthy, fit, trim people. We know that is not the case, and now we are beginning to understand why. It has not been and will not be the case unless and until we address the full dimensions of what we finally are recognizing as a major, growing, medical problem.

Remember, calories are energy units. You can expend them through exercise or put less or more of them into your body through eating. There are 9 calories per gram of fat (454 grams per pound). There are 4 - 5 calories per gram of carbohydrates and protein. There are then about 3500 calories per pound. "Do the math." If you eat about 2500 calories per day and you want to lose 1 pound per week, you less your days calories by 500 (7 x 500 = 3500). If you want to lose 2 pounds per week you eat 1000 fewer calories per day or expend that in energy with exercise, That would be 7000 caories per week or 2 pounds. (Thanks to Michael DeDoncker, Health and Sports Editor at the "Rockford Register Star" for this simple calculation.)

In summary, you can do the "exchange list" thousand calorie diet; you can follow a written 1000 calorie "menu"; you can "count" the calories by knowing what calories are in the food you eat; or you can go to "Jenny

Craig" or "Seattle Sutton" for your food in seperate packets for the day or week. All these ways are ok. Just so you keep those calories regulated.

Another important consideration is exercise, the subject of our next chapter. How vital is exercise to overcoming our weight control problems? It is absolutely essential to an effective, enduring diet program. Dr. Lamm agrees. He said that, when he returns calls, to answer a question for his weight management patients, he asks them, "Are you still exercising?" When they say, "Yes," he knows they are maintaining their weight loss.

Patient's Personal Comments

"I was a disbeliever at first - not any more! Eating is no longer a constant thought. I feel free; I can make choices, have control. It no longer controls me. Thank you so much!"

"Before I met Dr. Darland I tried just about every diet. I was always hungry. I used to eat a Lean Cuisine entree and have to have a salad and bread with it. Now on this medication I eat only the Lean Cuisine and sometimes I can't even finish!"

Notes:

Notes:

Chapter Five

In this chapter we will deal with another vital element in wellness through weight control. You will learn why and how all of us need to exercise - aerobically and isotonically - to achieve and maintain freedom from obesity. Exercise saves us from many unnecessary afflictions, which sideline and even kill the sedentary. You will learn that getting the exercise you need is simple and inexpensive. Many everyday exercise opportunities are free!

Patient's Personal Comments

"Now exercise is more than a chore. I can see results fast!"

rcise - Who Needs it?
We All Do.

ercise is as important a human function as eating."

Those are not the words of some modern American exercise guru. They are the words of Thomas Jefferson, perhaps the greatest apostle of freedom for all time and an inspiration for us in many areas, including diet and exercise. George Wills calls him "The person of the Millennium".

I know you may be surprised to find Thomas Jefferson quoted in a chapter on exercise, but I never intended to write just another diet and exercise book like the hundreds, maybe thousands, you can find on library and bookstore shelves. I write as a family doctor, sharing with you some stories and personal experiences that carry important messages for you and your life.

Jefferson, by the way, approached diet and exercise just as he approached everything else in his life - very thoughtfully and definitively. His daily diet was mostly fruits and vegetables, "With meat as a condiment." And exercise was an integral part of his entire life. Jefferson ran one mile out of Williamsburg to a big boulder and back several times a week when he was a college student. When he retired from his second presidential term, he would ride three to four hours each day on horseback. Even at age sixty-nine, with his leg feebled by arthritis, he walked as much as a mile a day. He and his peers, even centuries ago, knew well the value of exercise.

They knew it then and we know it now. So how did we Americans get into such poor shape? And what can we do about it?

Exercise, after all, is not complicated. The basics are summarized in two words: isotonics and aerobics. Isotonics are tension exercises we do with machines and barbells, dumbbells, and the free stationary-type floor exercises, such as sit-ups or push-ups. Aerobics, which literally means "with oxygen," are movement exercises. They include walking, running, biking, swimming, sustained "dance" type exercises done to music, and exercises on aerobic equipment, such as the Nordic Track and Cardio-glider, or even the modern "Tai-Bo" exercises.

Not only is exercise not complicated, but much of it also can be free!

Everyday life offers opportunities for walking and lifting and just plain moving. If you are one of the many developing sedentary, unhealthy, couch potato habits, change! Get off your behind. Do something. Move! You may even find more fun in your life! And your newfound fun may save your life.

As a child in Oskaloosa, Iowa, I was let out in the morning and called inside in the evening, about like the cows! We played in the barnyard, swam in the horse tank, and generally kept active, vigorously active, all day. There was no highly structured fun mixed with work.

Were we in good shape? I found the answer to that question in a dramatic way one spring day when our hundred acres were flooded. My big brother Rich and I were crossing a bridge over the brown, raging waters of our once small creek which had turned into an angry, foaming river.

I was standing on the edge of the old plank bridge looking down on the torrent when suddenly the plank end broke and I found myself in the water, flailing my arms against the swift current. I looked up at my big brother with what must have been a pretty terrified expression for a five-year-old boy.

Rich screamed for me to put my head down and swim for the side, which I did. Thank God for our days of barnyard play and our horse tank swimming exercises - and for my big brother Rich. That was the day I learned that exercise can save your life.

As a doctor, I know exercise can save your life in many other ways, also, including prevention of atherosclerotic and other degenerative diseases. And it can be fun for you.

I always played hard as a child, thanks to my family's enjoyment of baseball, tag football, roller-skating, ice-skating, and other games and activities requiring physical exertion. It wasn't until I was fourteen though, when I bought my first York barbell set with my newspaper delivery money, that I got serious.

I went out for Track and Basketball in grade school and High School, then joined the YMCA staff, which gave me free use of all the facilities. My buddies and I weight lifted, boxed, did gymnastics, wrestled, swam and were generously instructed by some of the greats in physical culture. I remember hearing Tony Zale, who traded off the Middle-weight World Championship with Rocky Graziano, and a famous strongman named Walter Brandt, who was able to lift seventeen people off a platform rig with his back and legs. He coached me to third place in the A.A.U. Pre Olympic weight lifting championships in northern Illinois. It was a great feeling.

About that time, the Korean War, or so-called "police-action" was heating up and I found myself at the top of the draft list with one of my buddies. My big brother Rich was already a sergeant with the 505th Infantry of the 82nd Airborne Division, so we joined the 82nd.

The 82nd was an outfit which emphasized exercise. Basic training and "jump school" were very vigorous. Our cadre officer, corporals, and sergeants were like demons from hell. They made us run everywhere. Ultimately, the exercise became exhilarating and even fun. Some of my buddies and I would actually go on our own runs because it felt good and we took pride in our running accomplishments.

We had a big gym on all the bases, and I kept up the barbells and dumbbells I had started with my York set at age fourteen. We would have push-up and pull-up contests on our own, as well as prepare for the required physical fitness test. In short, we were a very fit bunch.

I was married six months before the end of my three-year army hitch and was offered a promotion and chance to become a helicopter pilot if I would re-enlist, but decided against it. I wanted to start college, raise my family, and begin a career in YMCA work. That summer before school I started as a YMCA swim and gym instructor. After my first semester in school, I changed my goal to medicine with an emphasis on fitness and preventive medicine.

I worked with the YMCA for four years and at other jobs, which gave me a good base for my future work as a family doctor. In addition to being a swim and gym instructor, I later became a YMCA weight lifting instructor and worked out with classes on Monday and Thursday nights. We did an isotonic workout with the barbells and with free exercises, push-ups, and sit-ups. After that, we ran a mile or swam a quarter mile for aerobic power or "for the circulation," as we sometimes called it.

My commitment to a career in medicine and fitness, with deep appreciation for and understanding of the role of exercise, was bolstered by my YMCA experiences. I found the exercise ramifications of one program particularly important.

Thomas Cureton, a Ph.D. from the University of Illinois, gave our adult "Y" men a seminar on building strength and respiration-circulation fitness. I remember a study he described in which dogs had a coronary artery tied off and, after recovery, were put on a treadmill over some weeks. they were then compared to another group which had an artery tied off, but did not get any exercise.

The exercising dogs had a cascade, plexus "route-around" development of arteries that opened up with exercise to supply the heart muscle below the tied off obstruction. What Dr. Cureton and his researchers were describing for the first time was "collateral circulation post obstruction." Dr. Cureton cited this process as what happens most probably in humans who have obstruction. Indeed, we have since demonstrated that phenomenon.

I was impressed by this evidence of exercise helping the body heal itself, but I also was very impressed by the superb personal fitness of this sixty-year-old, gray-haired, barrel-chested teacher who obviously practiced what he preached.

I was his greeter and helper and host for that seminar. The night before the seminar he swam for his aerobic workout. And he swam and he swam and he swam. I was amazed. The next day he started by demonstrating strength and flexibility exercises and testing. After that, we retired to the pool for aerobics and he challenged the fit and interested "Y" adults of the city to swim the Olympic-sized pool length (75 feet) underwater, then walk to the other end and repeat it until the last swimmer was out. He and I were left. After the 26th lap, he whispered to me, "Do you want to call a draw?" I agreed. After all, he was only 60 and I was 25!

In medical school, I kept up my exercise as time allowed. I would study in the basement until I started to fall asleep, then I would go over to the furnace and "pump iron" for about twenty minutes, go out the back door of our English basement apartment in the Chicago Austin area, run about a mile, and come back and study for another hour. I walked to work three nights a week for the night shift at West Suburban Hospital in Oak Park and I would walk and take stairs whenever I could.

Part of my interest in preventive medicine and the role of exercise in maintaining health probably resulted from family experiences, also. I had two uncles who had died in their fifties of heart attacks and another uncle who survived a heart attack in his fifties. My revered grandfather died in his mid-sixties of generalized arteriosclerosis with stroke and heart disease. I can remember a time when I was young that I went to the neighborhood general store with my grandfather and he wanted cigarettes. He tried to tell the anxious, young female clerk that he wanted Camels, but his aphasia wouldn't allow him to articulate it. He was so angry and I was so saddened and upset that I started to cry.

I had my grandfather and uncles in mind when, as a medical student, I had a private interview with Dr. Mark Lepper, Professor of Health and Preventive Medicine at the University of Illinois College of Medicine. I asked Dr. Lepper, "If one would exercise vigorously and continuously all of his life, could he prevent a heart attack and prevent arteriosclerosis?" He answered, "I think there are a lot of related factors, but exercise is very important."

When I graduated from medical school, I was one of the 10% of graduates who wanted to be general practitioners. I kept my personal and medical interest in overall fitness and exercise. I still ran outside several days every week, starting when I was an intern and continuing the running when I went into private practice. I also sought and took steps to foster fitness in my Rockford, Illinois, home region and nationally.

In 1967, a friend, Sherwood Anderson, and I started the Rockford Road Runners. Later our Road Runners group sponsored "Fitness Day in Rockford" with a mayoral proclamation and special guest Ken Cooper, author of the book, <u>Aerobics</u>. Dennis Johnson, our alderman, gave Dr. Cooper the key to our city. Cooper spoke to seven different groups, including our hospital staff and the Sundstrand Corporation, an early advocate of employee fitness with a commitment, which included a fitness center and a full-time director.

In 1968, George Sheehan, Larry Lawrence, and I founded the American Medical Association's American Jogger's Association, in Central Park, New York to encourage physicians to get involved. To be truly effective, we doctors need to practice what we preach and do what we can to further wellness in our own communities.

In 1977, our hospital started the "Gold Medal Annual Run. " I was the race director the first year and we had the great marathoner Frank Shorter as our feature runner. He gave a talk the night before, visited the hospital to encourage a little boy with cystic fibrosis, and came over to our house to work out for a while in my home-gym. Frank said that even then, more and more runners were realizing the beneficial effects of weight training.

I ran in thirty-five marathons, including three Boston Marathons, in 17 years, starting at age 34. I also became more active in weight lifting and won third place in the Jim Swanson Midwest Open Power Lifting contest.

Through all this time I have been practicing medicine every day, trying to help my patients who want to lose weight and get fit. I recommend and encourage them to use what I call the three and three routine: three days of aerobics, three days of isotonics. The programs are highly variable, adapted to fit the specific needs of each patient but I insist on the principle that exercise is essential and that every patient must do some measure of it, both aerobic and isotonic.

As I mentioned before, you will find bookstore and library shelves packed with aerobic instruction books. For istonic exercise,

I, like Dr. Lamm, think the best book on the topic is *Getting Stronger*, written by Bill Pearl and Gary Moran, Ph.D. For women, I think the best book is *Body Shaping*, by Michael Yessis, Ph.D., the Women's Olympic Volleyball Team coach.

I am sometimes asked the question, "What about women and exercise?" The question often stems from myths and fears that exercise is somehow unfeminine or that it will masculinize women. What baloney! With good aerobic and isotonic workouts, girls and women only become more attractive and fit, with their beautiful musculature enhanced with more graceful lines and symmetry.

When I started as a YMCA physical education instructor, there were no women doing aerobic and isotonic exercise. That has now changed drastically for the good and women are participating in virtually all sports: cross-country running, power lifting, track, basketball, volleyball, and so on. Their beauty has been enhanced by their activity, not diminished. The only practice I discourage is the use of steroids. I think they can be very harmful. They also distort and masculinize the female form.

In aerobics, I instruct my patients, men and women, to get 30 Cooper points per week. That is based on Ken Cooper's quantitative advice on what variety and how much to do of each aerobic work out. I also advise motion extenders: walk when you can, lift when you can, etc. My advice is not only to do as much exercise as is necessary, but to do as much as you can.

In isotonics, I instruct my patients, men and women, to "pump iron," do machines, or do both. A barbell, dumbbell set is not expensive, and it is very durable. My step-father, at age 80, still used my York barbell set that I acquired at age fourteen.

Optimally in weight lifting, I advise four sets of ten repetitions each of the curl, uprightpress, bench-press, squat and bent-over rowing. Those five exercises are key to the essential overall body workout. I instruct my patients to get some form of them, such as barbells, dumbbells, or machines, three times per week.

My wife, Karen, was a body building competition champion. She works out regularly and vigorously every week. She is 5'2" and weighs 105 pounds. She has a body of a 16 year old and she's earned it. Karen is the business manager of my private family practice and has been an invaluable help and inspiration not only to me, but also to my patients. I often find myself telling patients, "There's Karen. She does this or that," and I show them her pictures and trophies. She and our office staff help keep our weight-reduction-fitness patients motivated with their example and enthusiasm. Motivation and support and encouragement are important, as we shall discuss in later chapters.

Exercise is very important in your weight reduction. Experience has confirmed that expression that "exercise not only adds life to your years, but years to your life!"

I want to tell you about another book, <u>Fitness is Religion</u> by Ray Kybartis, Simon & Schuster, 1997, forwarded by "Madonna"; our own American "Diva", who is one of his clients.

Mr. Kybartas uses this title as a metaphor to the fact that you must become committed to exercise, then you faithfully practice it for all its wonderful natural benefits - it's a good book.

George Sheehan wrote, <u>The Running Life</u>, another excellent book of the same vein. I ran with George in Central Park in 1968. He felt that with running, after you become fit, you could experience that almost religious feeling of being one with nature and god. He was quite an inspiration and still is in his legacy and books.

Taking advantage of what might be called environmental exercise opportunities - climbing steps instead of riding on escalators and elevators, carrying grocery bags to the car instead of wheeling them in a cart, for example

- can help control weight and also can help to prevent other ailments and miseries. According to Temple University's Dr. "Temple" Burney, strengthening exercises of the chest and back, flattening exercises, squats, and sit-ups can maintain the musculature which otherwise might no longer be adequate to support a man's or womans weight in an upright position. He cites weakness as one of the most common causes of low back pain and feels that exercise may drastically reduce the pharmaceutical approach to minimizing back pain.

I started this chapter by quoting Thomas Jefferson and referring to his lifelong devotion to human freedom. Exercise is a path to freedom from many unnecessary afflictions which sideline and even kill the sedentary. And exercise is absolutely essential to achieving and maintaining freedom from obesity. All of us need to exercise - constantly, aerobically and isotonically.

Jefferson also pointed out that no one in the midst of abundance has ever regretted eating too little. Many, on the other hand, have regretted eating too much. Ways to avoid that are the subject of our next chapter on what is sometimes called behavior modification.

Notes:

Notes:

Patient's Personal Comments

"The program is easy and hunger is a thing of the past. No side effects, just more energy from healthy food and exercise that I couldn't do before the program."

"I generally had been walking and lifting, alternating days during Monday through Thursday. I now walk, ride my bike and still lift, alternating days throughout the week if I miss a night, I do it the next day. I'm stiff and can feel the stress in my shoulders. I exercised because I had to; now I exercise because I want to!"

Chapter Six

In this chapter, you will learn that you must change some of your habits so you do more of what helps you and less or none of what hurts you. I will outline and elaborate on what I call the "four pillars" which underlie successful weight control programs. The medication helps you modify your behavior and your behavior modification in turn helps the medication do its work. Together they help you reach your goal of fit and healthy living.

Patient's Personal Comments

"The days in my work week are so hectic that when it came time for me to eat I would just grab a candy bar or stop at a fast food place. My weight kept going up and I found myself worrying constantly about how big I was getting. This put more pressure on me. A friend of mine told me about you and the Phen-Xen program, Dr. Darland. I've lost 24 pounds so far and I noticed I feel better, I can even handle the stress of work without feeling I need to have food for comfort. I'm taking time to treat myself as someone important. "

Behavior Modification

Behavior modification is a term coined by psychiatrists, psychologists, rehabilitative medical specialists, sociologists, and others. In corrective and preventive medicine, it simply means changing your habits so you do more of whatever helps you and less or none of whatever hurts you.

Behavior modification in weight reduction and fitness means developing good eating, exercise, and mental habits. What specifically?

I explain in my patient orientations that there are four foundations for a good, successful weight loss and fitness program.

First, you must be motivated, that is, you have to be *ready*, resolved, determined, and committed.

Second, you must follow a *diet*.

Third, you must eat foods *low in fat*.

Fourth, you must *exercise*.

Those are what I call the "four pillars," like the four comers of a structure, providing the foundation for a platform on which to stand. Often I draw this in four Doric columns, put a platform on the columns, and draw a quick sketch depicting the patients with their arms outstretched overhead in a symbol of victory.

I explain that diet is the most critical pillar of all and emphasize that losing weight and maintaining fitness demand a change in eating patterns and habits. To illustrate, I draw a house, put in windows and a door, put a roof and chimney on it, and explain that, just as builders must have plans for building a house, we must have a plan for building a new body. The diet is the plan, the outline, the guide too new eating behavior.

I outline specific eating behavior with usually no more than 1000 calories per day and give the diet to insure intelligent food selection. I have patients count calories, sometimes just for one to two weeks of the months interval between doctor visits. I strictly admonish no "in-betweens" and no "seconds." I don't like the carrot stick snack or juice break or any calories in between; zero, nothing caloric. That's my style and reasonably it prevents overeating.

Eating behavior modification means no candy bar, no vending machine stops, no pop, nothing while you are on your diet. I also advise fasting one full day per week and missing two major meals per week, both of which are okay for most of my patients. Your doctor will note any restrictions and advise you in your specific case.

I know it may sound to you as though the 82nd Airborne sergeant in me is coming out here, but we have to stick to the plan in order to achieve our mission. The medication helps, but does not work by itself. You must modify your eating habits in line with the plan. The medication makes it a little easier to make the changes, but it is your eating behavior modification itself, which will guarantee success.

Although I encourage you to be strong and adopt these and other changes, I also want to caution you not to be too hard on yourself if you "fall off." That itself can lead to bingeing. Just get up, dust yourself off, and start all over again. Be realistic and remember you are working to change habits that have developed and solidified over a lifetime. It is like fighting a big bully. Congratulate and encourage yourself for the fight you are waging, focus on your victories, and resolve to stay on course.

Focusing on victories and resolving to stay on course are helpful in overcoming built in obstacles we are just beginning to understand. One of those obstacles has been cited by Dr. Sarah Leibovich, a researcher at the Rockefeller Institute in New York City, who suggest that some of us may have appestats which do not work well. The appestat is defined as an area of the brain, in the hypothalamus, which is thought to control appetite and food intake. Some persons' neuropeptides may be chemically different and may block transmission of the message to stop eating. That is just one more example of the complexity of obesity and of how our nature can work against even our best intentions and efforts. The innumerable medical, psychological, and physiological factors contributing to obesity and overweightness help us understand why the challenge is so great and why behavior modification is so essential. Behavior modification means changing our ways and doing what we can to make our nature work for us instead of against us. Phen-Xen provides powerful medical assistance and can make the difference *if* you are motivated and ready, follow the diet, eat foods low in fat, and exercise.

Occasionally I will add Prozac to the regimen. This helps further to control the appetite urgings and cravings. If we use all three medicines, we call it the "Phen/Xen/Pro" program. When I counsel changing your ways to make your nature works for you instead of against you, I am giving a guideline you must apply in the specific circumstances of your life. Keeping a diet diary will help you see and avoid some of the environmental eating triggers in your life. Examine your eating pitfalls over a period of weeks and take steps to avoid the causes and circumstances. Be creative in your approaches and do not hesitate to ask others for help. You can find thousands of ideas in bookstores and libraries, though you probably need to make only a few changes.

Dr. Gerald Hoffman, psychiatrist in private practice in Rockford, Illinois, was a resident at the University of Illinois Medical School in Chicago, Illinois. He was a student of the noted Psychiatrist Beulah Bossleman, author and head of the department of Psychiatry at the University of Illinois in Chicago, and was then known as the "Hub of Freudian Psychiatry," according to Dr. Hoffman. Dr. Hoffman was one of my teachers then, and has been one of my revered mentors ever since.

Recently at the Rockford YMCA, Dr. Hoffman (he is a very fit Psychiatrist) and I discussed this aspect of the book; behavior modification, medicine, and a better lifestyle.

He feels that with the constancy of better habits not only does the personality regulate to this better lifestyle, but there is some evidence that physiologically our chemical humoral brain metabolism may change and adapt to this good behavioral modification - fascinating! But sometimes we do need the help of medicine like Prozac. Dr. Leland Heller, M.D., elucidates many of these ideas in his excellent book, *Biological Unhappiness*, an excellent expository book that talks about anxiety, depression, obsessive-compulsive disease, bipolar disorder, ADD, ADHD, borderline personality, sociopathic personality, panic attacks and other very common psychological, physiological problems; including overeating disorder.

A comical but effective example illustrates how behavior modification can be put to work in making our circumstances propel us toward our goal. Imagine a man who wants to get up at 6 a.m., but never makes it. He decides to create a motivator to get himself out of bed when the alarm goes off. He attaches his alarm to a device which tips a pan of water pre-set to splash on his face a few seconds after the alarm goes off .He forgets and gets drenched the first day, but from then on he jumps up immediately to stop the water splash. His fast response is behavior modification at work for him. We put it to work for us by changing or creating circumstances which help us develop the habit of doing what is best for us, even though there are very, very powerful forces working against us every step of the way.

One of the most powerful forces working against some patients and what may be one of the greatest contributors to obesity is behavior classified as obsessive compulsive disorder (O.C.D.). In weight problems, the disorder is characterized by persons using food as tranquilizers to allay anxiety and to quell whatever emotional difficulties they may be experiencing. Potent power though it may be, the O.C.D. problem can be conquered. I have many patients receive help from psychiatrists because they have been unable to handle their urgings alone without counseling and medicine.

Interestingly food may raise serotonin levels in the brain. Prozac is better.

It is my opinion, based on experience and research, that there are gradations to O.C.D. One person may eat minimally in between meals, but be unable to resist the compulsion to ask for a second helping of goulash, for example. Some patients have a very serious problem, as does one of my patients who weighs more than 400 pounds and has had grave medical problems, including a pulmonary embolus (blood clot) that could have been fatal. His typical behavior would include going to the store to pick up an item for his wife, stopping at a fast food drive-through and buying eight hamburgers which he would eat before going home, then sitting down to eat his usual supper. He said he would respond to any problems with the children after supper by returning to the kitchen and gorging himself into psychological satiety. I say psychological because he said to me during his hospitalization, "I am never hungry, I just eat." The patient is now making good strides with the help of his psychiatrist, the nutritionist, the pastor at his church, and me.

I recently received encouragement for my O.C.D. patients at a Virginia Beach conference on "Family Practice Problems - A Review." One of the preceptors, a psychiatrist practicing in Washington D.C., cited SSRI's like Luvox and Prozac as an effective medication for helping patients with O.C.D. The medicine can be partner medications to Phentermine and Xenical in treating the overweight problem itself, like the Phen/Xen/Pro approach. Dr. Michael Anchors, M.D. of Georgetown University wrote an excellent book titled Safer Than Phen/Fen where he advocated Phen/Pro, August, 1997.

The behavior modification aspect of dealing with obesity in these and less severe situations is very important. Its importance is brought home in the unfortunate story of another patient who is in prison right now. before being incarcerated, she had been unable to get off the last 30 pounds she needed to lose. We write periodically, and she recently told my wife Karen and me that she is now normal weight, finally losing those 30 pounds in the restricted environment of the prison. That is doing it the hard way, but her experience further illustrates the power of behavior modification.

All four factors are important to achieving normal weight and fitness:

- Motivation, that is, being ready, resolved, determined, committed.

- Following a diet.

- Eating foods low in fat.

- Exercising.

Behavior modification ties them all together. The medication helps to modify behavior and the behavior modification in turn helps the medication do its work. All together they help us overcome the obstacles to fit and healthy living.

There are other obstacles we must overcome, also. I call them the saboteurs. We will discuss them in the next chapter.

Notes:

Notes:

Patient's Personal Comments

"Being on this program, I feel for the first time 'normal.' I have energy and am enthusiastic. I have some control! I can now choose whether I really want something instead of eating it and knowing later I didn't really need or want it."

"Recording everything I was consuming - even those items that were supposed to be diet foods - was an awakening for me. I found there are some things, i.e., prime rib, I will probably never eat again. I don't look at this plan as a diet! It's really not. It is a behavior modification. I used to eat because it was time to eat or I was bored and had nothing else to do. It was a reward' for myself, a friend. Now I stay so busy I don't even realize I've missed lunch. I can pass the box of donuts at the office. I don't stop to smell them, look at them, or eat them now."

Chapter Seven

In this chapter you will learn about people who consciously or unconsciously try to undermine your efforts and how you can overcome them. Some saboteurs are well intentioned but misguided people, including some who are close to you. Others may be people you see every day who are threatened by your success and become the victims of their insecurity. I will warn you about the destructive dynamics at work and help you fortify yourself against the saboteurs' tricks and temptations.

Patient's Personal Comments

"I've never been happier, more energetic and self-confident. I have a strong family history of heart disease, cancer, high blood pressure and diabetes on both sides. Being a nurse, I've always been conscious of my health and try to take care of myself and family by eating right and staying active. The Phen/Xen program has made it so easy! I've had a few Saboteurs since starting the program; telling me I was losing the weight too fast and wanting to know if I was taking those 'speed' pills some people take to lose weight. I assured them I was not, but you know how some people talk I have recommended this program to several friends and they too, are having success in their weight loss. I just hope more physicians start prescribing this program to their patients and give them the support I have received form Dr. Darland and staff. My husband and children love the new person I've become and I am so proud of the new me!"

Sometimes they do it subtly.

Sometimes they do it blatantly.

Sometimes they do it unconsciously.

Sometimes they do it by malicious design.

What do they do?

They sabotage your diet efforts.

Webster's Dictionary defines sabotage as a treacherous action to defeat or hinder a cause or endeavor.

Who are "they" and how do they do it?

"They" can be your spouse, you parents, your friends, your co-workers, our classmates, your church associates, or anyone you meet. "They" can even be well intentioned but misguided medical or media professionals.

First they tell you that diet, per se, is bad. Or they say your doctor is just not with it. "You go to him/her? You're taking diet pills? Those pills are bad for you. You must be crazy. Those are 'street drugs' you know."

Some start in with "You look sick. Do

you feel okay? Don't you think you're losing too fast? One day off your diet isn't going to matter. You need that food for your body."

Others say, "You know you are just going to gain it all right back. Diets don't work." And they refer to someone you both know who tried and failed. "Remember Jane Doe who lost fifty pounds? Now she has gained it all back and then some."

Sometimes it takes the form of food or candy as a present from someone who knows you are dieting. Someone brings brownies to the office and says, "One isn't going to hurt you."

They are among all of us all the time. They are people who have a penchant for destroying the dieter, subtly or blatantly, unconsciously or by design.

Some husbands, for example, become fearful when their wives begin to look as attractive as they did on their wedding nights. Husbands who have this insecurity become what I call "saboteurs." I believe there are more husbands in this category than there are wives who sabotage their husbands' weight loss.

Friends, even friends who are not overweight themselves, can feel threatened by your emerging new body and your new self-mastery. After all, they have always had the upper hand in being trim and looking better in their clothes than you. They have become accustomed to getting more compliments and can feel threatened when others take note of your new, more attractive appearance.

I have observed all of these situations in my practice. I feel that our loved ones want us to succeed, but they become the victims of basic and strong psychological defense mechanisms common to all, even when they love us and have high regard for us.

So be ready to deal with the saboteurs in your relationships. Stay on course yourself and try to find ways to help them deal with what may be serious psychological challenges for them.

An example of the types of responses I am describing comes from one of my patients who lost forty pounds on her 5'2" medium frame and looked beautiful. She exercised the whole time and her renewed enthusiasm and "joie de vivre" were very evident in her new, vivacious, attractive self. She was noticed and complimented by a friend at her church. The friend was an older, overweight woman who asked, "How did you do it?" My patient told me that she described her weight loss program to her friend, but noticed a change in her friend's mood as she talked about the program. The woman's enthusiastic curiosity gave way to what my patient described as a "glaze." An expressionless, calculated indifference came over her. That was followed by a frown and the comment, "Well, you'll probably just gain it all back. " She then turned and walked away without so much as a simple good-bye.

That is how the saboteurs do it to you.

Much of this saboteur business is the big, "Green Monster" - envy. It is the "have/have not" syndrome. It is the pointing out to others what they themselves have not been able to do, sometimes after great effort, and they resent it. I tell my patients, though, not to despair. Envy is often the highest expressed form of admiration. Take it graciously, with a smile.

Another underlying cause of sabotage is what I call the "Don't change, I like you as your are" syndrome. It often is an expression of fear stemming from insecurity. Your spouse says, "I want a girl just like the girl that married dear old dad. Sure, she was fat, but she was my mom and I loved her. I was comfortable and secure with her." You are supposed to be obese just because someone's parents were? Baloney!

The saboteurs mean well for the most part. They simply cannot help themselves at this point. They may be as victimized by their fears as you have been by your weight problem, so be charitable and understanding and forgiving. Most important of all, do not become a victim with them. Be aware of the dynamics at work and do not give in to the tricks and temptations. Remember, it is their problem, not yours. You know weight loss and fitness are right for you, good for you, healthy for you, so be confident and stay on course.

You also may meet saboteurs in the medical professions, physicians and pharmacists who are not educated and current on the facts from research work on this approach. They are hypercritical of patients, doctors, and others involved in this new, successful medical treatment for obesity.

This does not mean the detractors are not well meaning persons. With the history of fad diets, diet pills, and the abject failure of obesity treatment in the past, it is easy to understand their criticism and concern for even the most minuscule and rare of side effects. They frighten the uninformed, who seem to forget that even simple cough drops and candy can have side effects, also minuscule and rare. They seem to forget that eating food can make you feel good and can cause a serotonin increase in the brain, also, just as the medication does. The only difference is that the food makes you fat and the medicine does not. On the contrary, the medication helps you get thinner and healthier. Their groundless fears and unfounded allegations ignore the risk to benefit ratio which compels informed, clear thinking persons to acknowledge the urgency of treating obese patients, both to save their lives and to improve the quality of their lives.

The sabotage we encounter today is, in my judgement, nothing less than a form of discrimination. Obese patients, after all, have rights, too. For too long, obese patients have been treated as though they were somehow responsible for their condition. For too long, obese patients have been admonished to change a condition they are essentially powerless to change. As another doctor has pointed out, simply telling patients to lose weight in many cases is like instructing patients to have a spontaneous remission of cancer. Yes, spontaneous remissions of cancer do happen, but that certainly does not mean we should withdraw the support of medical science from the treatment of cancer - or obesity. The informed now know that obesity is a medical problem we can treat. But to treat it effectively, we need to have the same sympathy and understanding in treating obesity as we do in treating other diseases. We need to give patients hope and encouragement for a better and longer life. And we need to give them the same benefits of medical science we give others.

Some patients may have to use the medication intermittently and with varying dosages all their lives. Others may not. The medication may be just an adjunct to a new life style of increased attention to nutrition, exercise, and other new habits. It can be likened to the treatment now common for reducing or eliminating 95 percent of the devastating effects most often associated with adult type diabetes mellitus. Or it can be likened to the lifesaving treatment now common for hypertensive patients.

I believe that in about five years we will

no longer have to deal with sabotage by professionals. By then, prescribing medication to treat obesity will be as natural and common for doctors as prescribing medication for diabetes and hypertension is today. In the meantime, let us move forward to help everyone we can.

The sabotage problem is so difficult for many patients that I include it in the materials I give them and always discuss it with them personally at the start of the program. It is very important to know how to deal with your loved ones and friends during the dieting. After I do the history and physical, I often say, "You know, sometimes it is best to do this on your own in a personal and private way because there are going to be 'saboteurs' out there. You're going to run into roadblocks and potholes on your road to normal weight that you don't need to run into. So be prepared to deal with it. You can explain to others what you are doing. You can confront them and put them in their place. Or you can just keep still and do as Henry Ford said, "Don't complain and don't explain.'"

Another approach you can use is the powerful achiever technique called the "buddy system."

If you know someone who will help you, who will be of good cheer and support you, you have someone who can make an important contribution to your success. It may be a husband or wife, a mother or father, a brother or sister, or a dear friend.

You will find a way. I know you will or you would not have read this far. You are the captain of your own ship, the master of your own destiny. Watch out for and never surrender to the saboteurs. A powerful help is a positive, healthy philosophy. That is the subject of our next chapter.

Notes:

Notes:

Notes:

Patient's Personal Comments

"Another form of sabotage is the 'holier than thou attitude of 'I did it without medication. I have self-control, why don't you?' And, 'What kind of doctor would prescribe diet pills these days?' For a person with low self-esteem because of weight, these types of comments can be discouraging. Since I've been on the program and have seen visible success (as my skeptics have also noticed), the superiority attitude doesn't bother me anymore."

"I worked with a woman who was so wrapped up by her looks and physique that all she talked about was 'Oh, look at me, I gained two pounds, I've got to go on a diet again!' I tell you, I got so sick of hearing that I was to the point I stopped complimenting her on her looks and shape. She couldn't take a compliment or just wanted attention, I'm not sure which. When I'd lose some weight and people noticed, she would also comment. After lunch she always returned with a little

something from the bakery. She'd put it on my desk and say 'You deserve it, you've done so well.' I'd eat it. If someone complimented me on my success and asks any questions, she'd come up to us and the conversation always reverted back to her. For seven years we went through this. She's taken a job elsewhere and it's nice. I don't have to worry any longer. Are you sick, you look anorexic, are you OK ?' The compliments are genuine now. Mom was much the same way - 'eat, you're too skinny, are you sick?' No more. I've got control."

Chapter Eight

In this chapter, you will learn that a healthy personal philosophy provides you with added power and strength for reaching your goal and staying there. Your philosophy helps you understand yourself better and makes you more persistent in doing what is best. When you have a clear picture of who you are and what you are and what your purpose in life is, you are more likely to succeed.

Patient's Personal Comments

"Thank you for giving me the tools to make my lifestyle changes in my eating habits and' helping me use those tools as a stepping stone toward a healthier and positive me. When I came to Dr. Darland, I wasn't even sure this was what I wanted. Could it be a fix-all with no discipline needed? If it didn't take some sort of discipline, i.e., exercise, etc., I didn't want it. I knew after being on many diets, the weight eventually comes back to haunt you. I am a 30 year old female who comes from a background of bouts with depression and low self-image. The program is wonderful and I feel very proud of myself to maintain and go on with my life feeling good and projecting confidence. That's what is important to me, not just the pounds coming off but just feeling good about me."

Philosophy - Who Needs It?
We All Do.

What is this - a chapter on philosophy in a book about losing weight? What does philosophy have to do with it? How can it help you reach your goal?

Well, the word "philosophy" comes from the Greek words "philia," meaning "to love," and "sophia," meaning "wisdom." So philosophy means love of wisdom. Webster defines wisdom as a search for truth through logical reasoning encompassing all learning. We say someone has wisdom when he or she understands something, knows the right thing to do, and does it.

In previous chapters, you acquired a kind of wisdom about weight problems. You understand the causes and the cure. You know the right things to do in diet, exercise, behavior modification, and how to handle saboteurs. You know about the added power medication can provide.

But there is another power you must have. And that is where philosophy comes in. I am talking about your personal philosophy, your worldview, your "Weltanschauung," as the German philosophers call it. It is my contention that your personal philosophy, your "Weltanschauung," can provide you with added power to drive the task, make you more forceful, more persistent, and more likely to succeed.

It is not my goal here to tell you what to think. My goal is to encourage you to think. English author George Bernard Shaw, whose delightful story "Pygmalion" became the musical production "My Fair Lady," said, "Most people never think, I think five minutes each year and it has made me famous." Thinking, real thinking, is not as common as you might expect.

Consider the amount of time many Americans spend watching television, what TV critics and even some leaders in the TV industry have called "a vast mental wasteland" and "bubble gum for, the eyes." A recent study has reported that Americans spend an average of seven hours a day watching television. Just think of that! They are spending seven hours a day as passive, sometimes nearly mindless, couch potatoes. That same time could be spent in active pursuits, fostering a healthier body and mind.

As we ponder what some are now calling an epidemic of obesity in America, is it possible that there is a connection between unhealthy TV viewing habits and unhealthy living habits? Is it possible that there is a connection between mind-clogging TV and artery-clogging fat? Even television executives are telling Americans to cut back on TV and get a real life. Even TV industry ads are telling viewers to make time for reading and being physically active.

Think about it yourself. Just think. Does spending hours in front of a TV help you fulfill your destiny as a human being? Are you using and developing your full powers when you are planted in front of your television set, immobilized on your couch? Is that your destiny? Are you using and developing your full powers when you passively accept being told what to do and what to buy and what to think? Is that your destiny? Your answers to those questions depend on your philosophy, your worldview, and you cannot answer those questions - in words and actions - unless and until you have one.

Having your own philosophy can enable you to have a clear picture of who you are and what you are and what your purpose in life is. Having your own philosophy can help you grow in wisdom as you understand yourself better, know what is best for you, and do what is best. Having your own philosophy can empower you to avoid and resist those who would reduce you to a mere statistic, a mere animal to be driven and manipulated.

Developing a healthy philosophy is a do-it-yourself project. Others can start you toward one. It starts to form as you learn from your parents, your grandparents, our teachers, friends, church and community leaders. It grows through your personal observations and experiences, through what you read and hear and see. But it does not become your own until you exercise our thinking powers, the powers which separate you from the plants and animals, your powers to analyze and synthesize.

I love and have been a student of philosophy since I began to think and read, to observe and experience. I named this chapter after a book by Ayn Rand, one of my favorite philosophers. She also wrote <u>Atlas Shrugged</u>, <u>Fountainhead</u> and <u>Anthem</u>, among other books.

I visited her Manhattan office at the Empire State Building in New York City and think of her as an admirable, devout American, whose philosophy is quite well-defined, as shown by her impressive work.

I think it is best to be organized and have a systematic approach to answering questions, which help form, a personal philosophy. Where do we fit in and what is our role? How do we learn? What is right and wrong? Those are some of the questions we ask. In her book by the same title as this chapter, Ayn Rand classifies philosophy into five general areas:

- Metaphysics, dealing with the question of "being" and "purpose;"

- Epistemology, the study of how we know, how we use our senses and power of reason to find real truth;

- Ethics or Axiology, the study of what is right and wrong, what our code of values should be as individuals, as parents, as friends or fellow workers, as citizens of our country and the world;

- Political Economy, the study of what is the best system by which humans can live with each other and with other life forms on the planet, the best system of government and how governmental laws match our rights in the so called free market system, and

- Aesthetics, the study of beauty and the arts which elevate us all to a feeling of Gods glory and grandeur.

"That is it," Ayn Rand says. "We all need to have a philosophy, to put ourselves in the perspective of a relationship with each and every one of these entities."

I agree.

Of course, your philosophy does not have to be as formally organized and presented as Ayn Rand's. I found a great illustration of a personal philosophy in a few lines from the John Wayne film, "The Shootist." In one of the scenes, Wayne and Ron Howard, who plays the teenage son of Wayne's adoring landlady, are sauntering down the dusty main street when Howard says, "Can I ask what your credo is?" A credo is what we are calling a philosophy or worldview. Wayne turns to Howard and says, "Well, son, it's simple. I won't be insulted. I won't be wronged. I won't be laid a hand on. I do that for others and I expect the same from them."

It was a beautiful, brief statement of a personal philosophy or world view. I thought to myself, where did I hear that before? From

grandma? From Reverend Randolph at the Presbyterian Church when I was a boy in Oswego, Illinois? From the wonderful Miss Brooks, my second grade teacher? From that high-up leader at the YMCA? From the current affairs educational corporal when I was in basic training?

I realized Wayne's credo came right out of that most revered library of books called The Bible. Wayne's character adopted and adapted it to make it his own. I have done something similar myself. The way I say it is, "Don't name-call; don't 'put-down'; don't use verbal or physical abuse; and practice the Golden Rule - do unto others as you would have them do unto you. "

My personal philosophy includes ideas about our nature. I believe in the virtually limitless capacity for expansion of human knowledge. I believe in the improvability of humankind. I believe all of us can learn and take advantage of advancing knowledge if we have an open mind. My philosophy embraces principles sacred to those who created our American experiment in self-government: belief in the worth of the individual, that the rights of humankind come from God, not from the state, and that those rights include the rights to life, liberty, and the pursuit of happiness. Those elements of my philosophy give me an understanding of myself and others and help me develop habits of body, mind, and soul to fulfill my destiny.

That is why your philosophy is so important. It helps you know who you are and what you are and what your destiny is, the fulfillment of your nature. Your body, for example, is designed to provide a certain optimum performance. That is its nature. A healthy philosophy helps you respect your body and treat it properly so it can give you the pleasure of its optimum performance.

Of course, an unhealthy philosophy can do just the opposite. Too often I see patients who are suffering, in part at least, from the natural effects of flawed philosophy. If a patient's "Weltanschauung" is unhealthy, it leads to unhealthy habits and outlook and attitude. Until that is changed, we can treat symptoms, but cannot restore the patient to full health.

Achieving and sustaining full health of body, mind, and soul is what your philosophy should be accomplishing for you. If ours is not, perhaps it is time to rethink it. It is most obvious, perhaps, in the body. If you have a person who cannot walk 50 feet without panting, or who does not have the, energy to do activities at night, who cannot take care of his or her children or job, or who is going to die half way through a normal life span because of obesity, that person is not able to really optimize and fulfill his or her destiny. I do not believe anyone can be totally, optimally fulfilled without a philosophy which puts body, mind, and soul in sync.

Fitness is not merely the absence of disease. It is the power to do things important to our roles in life as workers, spouses, parents, and citizens. It includes the power to get up, do your work, have fun, and play, all of which in turn rejuvenate and renew each other.

Of course, all of us inherit genetic dispositions and some have environmental influences beyond their control. Within the framework of each person's conditions, however, it is generally true that a healthy philosophy creates healthy thoughts which foster optimum health.

In my experience, when patients get their "Weltanschauung" corrected, when they feel organized and whole in regard to their philosophy of life, other things tend to fall into place a little better. When they are empowered with their own feeling of worth, their own value, and their own sense of a purpose and destiny, then they are more easily able to carry out the work they have to do to achieve their goals no matter how difficult the challenge and no matter how many saboteurs they encounter along the way.

We started this chapter on the role of your philosophy by noting that we call someone wise when he or she understands something, knows the right thing to do, and does it. That practical wisdom is illustrated by one of the great Olympic champion long distance runners from Finland, Paavo Nurmi, the winner of six gold medals and numerous other honors.

A mistake many runners make is paying too much attention to the competition and what is going on around them. They fail to pace themselves, expend too much energy at the wrong time, and come up short of the strength needed for a final burst of energy to propel themselves across the finish line to victory.

Nurmi's secret was to carry a stopwatch as he ran to check his performance against his stopwatch rather than against the competition. His stopwatch kept him focused on doing what he knew he needed to do to win, helped him to ignore distractions along the way, and helped him pace himself so he had the strength to cross the finish line and achieve his gold medal goals.

Your healthy personal philosophy is like Nurmi's watch. It can keep you focused, give you reassurance along the way, help you ignore any distraction and detraction you may encounter, and propel you across your finish line - gloriously victorious.

In the next chapter, we will take a closer look at some medical dimensions and complications of obesity, a rogue's gallery of miseries you are leaving behind as you win your long distance race to fitness.

Notes:

Notes:

Patient's Personal Comments

"My sister referred me to your program. Upon entering the program I felt terrible. Some days I didn't want to go on. With the willpower, determination, and the medicine I got a whole new outlook on my life."

"I have been on this program for three months now and have lost 35 pounds. I feel great about myself, I have more confidence in myself because I have improved my self-image. I have a goal of a total weight loss of 60-65 pounds. I feel confident that I can reach that goal. One of the hardest things for me to get used to is the compliments and attention I am receiving. It is different to have people see me as attractive. I have never received compliments like these before. I know I am improving my health, but the best improvement is my own self-image. I'm so glad I was introduced to this program."

Chapter Nine

In this chapter, you will learn about the growing list of afflictions and complications which accompany obesity. Bear in mind as you read that your primary care doctor now has an effective treatment and cure for obesity which can free you from those harmful effects.

Patient's Personal Comments

"As I watched my mother struggle with her overweightness, diabetes and heart disease, I realized I was watching my own future. Now with your help and the medical program I'm changing the future. Thank you!"

The Medical Hazards Of Obesity Or "How Bad Is It, Doctor?"

We now know that there are genetic, cultural, behavioral, socioeconomic, and situational factors contributing to the disease of obesity. It is the multiple combinations of those co-variables which make it extraordinarily difficult to assess the impact of any one factor alone and cause debates about the relative importance of each.

Though the causes may be debated, there is general agreement that obesity is harmful. I am sometimes asked, "How bad is it, Doctor?"

First, I set aside quibbling over definitions of the terms "obesity" and "overweightness." Body Mass Index aside, calipers aside, if you look fat, if you are at least 20% overweight, you are at risk.

For example, if you are a woman who should weigh 120 pounds and you weigh 145 pounds, you are at risk for the medical hazards of obesity. If you are a man who should weigh

165 pounds and you weigh 190, you are at risk for the major killing diseases: heart attacks, which cause 35% of deaths annually, hypertension, strokes, diabetes - ninety to ninety-five percent of which is Type II adult onset, and all the attendant complications of those grave diseases and more.

Another set of factors is onset and duration of obesity. Generally, if you are obese and young, and keep it longer, your hazards are much greater than if you become obese at an older age and have it for a shorter time. All Primary Care Doctors can relate to this easily among their own patients.

We are finding out more specifics on obesity and disease now and even have some estimates in percentages of patients' risks. Known disease risks include mainly the following:

1. Insulin resistance

2. Hypertension

3. Dyslipidemia

4. Cardiovascular disease

5. Non-Insulin-Dependent Diabetes Mellitus

6. Gall Stones and Cholycystitis (The "fair, fat and forty" syndrome)

7. Respiratory dysfunction (The Pickwickian Syndrome, decreased pulmonary function which means the lungs do not exchange oxygen and carbon dioxide as they do in healthy persons)

8. Certain forms of Cancer

Persons 20% overweight have a prevalence of hypertension twice that of persons of normal weight. In the western world, fully one-third of the cases of elevated blood pressure are thought to be due to obesity alone. In men younger than 45 years of age, the figure may reach 60%.

Elevated Lipids

In the Framingham Study, the most lengthy coronary study completed, every 10% increase in relative weight was associated with an increase in cholesterol of 12 milligrams. The increase of the ratio of HDL (high density lipoproteins, the "good cholesterol") to LDL (low density lipoproteins, the "harmful cholesterol") is generally higher, leading to a greater atherogenic risk. Pharmaceutical industry research reports tell us that for every 1% increase of total cholesterol there is a 2% increase in Coronary Artery Disease.

Coronary Heart Disease

Even mild to moderate overweight condition increases the risk of Coronary Artery Disease whether or not there are elevated lipids, as Jeremiah Stamler reports in his book _Your Heart Has Nine Lives_.

There is a significant trend toward increasing mortality rates with increasing Body

Mass Index for all end points studied, including both cancer and cerebrovascular death. This held true, also, in the Seventh Day Adventist nonsmoking group study and others, even with risk factors culled out. Moreover, obesity in and of itself is a risk factor for an earlier death. Dr. Xavier Pi-Sunger reported in his October of 1993 *Annals of Internal Medicine* paper, "Medical Hazards of Obesity," however, that the protective effect for those in the lowest 20% of Body Mass Index (low body weight) decreased with advancing age and disappeared by 90 years of age.

Diabetes Mellitus

Risk for Non-Insulin-Dependent Diabetes Mellitus is two times greater for the mildly obese who are 20% overweight. It is five times greater for the moderately obese who are 40% overweight, and ten times greater for the severely obese who are 60% overweight. A study in Scandinavia showed that even moderate obesity was associated with a ten-fold risk for Diabetes. Other factors, of course, are critical: family history, and so-called centrally located obesity, sometimes called the "apple" shape.

Gallbladder Disease

Gallbladder Disease is three to four times more likely in the obese, especially in women. It comes mostly in the form of cholesterol stones due to cholesterol super-saturation of the bile and a greater gallbladder stasis or stagnation of fluids there as obesity occurs.

Respiratory Disease

Decreased volume of air in the lungs and hypoxia or deficiency of oxygen available is a result of obesity and is observable in extreme Pickwickian Syndrome. As severity of obesity increases, so does sleep apnea syndrome, the periodic cessation of breathing during sleep. Cor Pulmonale, enlargement of the heart, also may occur as a result of the lung disorder. There is a 50% five-year death rate for

Pickwickianism. This may help to clear up some of the confusion generated by data regarding Primary Pulmonary Hypertension in the European experience with Redux, a medication that was caught up in what I call the "Phen-Fen" debacle.

Cancer

The American Cancer Society followed 750,000 men and women for twelve years. They found the obese have a significantly higher mortality rate for Colorectal and Prostate cancer. The mortality rate for men 40% or more overweight was 133% higher for both diseases and the mortality rate for overweight women was 155% higher for Colorectal. Women who were overweight also have significantly higher rates of Endometrial, Gallbladder, Cervical, Ovarian and Breast cancer. Obesity also is a factor in the breast cancer mortality rate in postmenopausal obese women, increasing in proportion to the degree of obesity.

Gout

Obesity contributes to an increased level of uric acid and frequent attacks of gout.

Arthritis

Osteoarthritis also increases with obesity, with incidence doubling in men and tripling in women according to Weber and Pi-Sunger.

I sometimes am asked, "What about where your fat is?" Even distribution is important. Using body shape description terms coined by Sheldon Levine, M.D., in his book The Redux Revolution, do you see yourself as a "pencil" or a "dirigible?" Are you a "pear" or and "apple?" There is an increase in the overall mortality rate with an increased abdominal, upper body fat, the so-called "apple" shaped fat. Visceral or "pear" shaped fat is lower risk than central fat, though still a greater risk than being fit and normal weight.

Central body fat or "apple" shaped fat also has a greater increased risk for high blood pressure, increased lipidemia, increased Cardiovascular Athersclerosis, increased Gallbladder ailments, and increased Diabetes Mellitus and insulin resistance. The increased incidence of Diabetes Mellitus is eight times greater with central body fat, according to the eight year Oheson Scandinavian prospective study of Generalized Adiposity (fat deposits) versus Central Adiposity.

In summary, obesity is bad for you. Age of onset, duration, physical fitness, location of fat, and other factors are important in determining how bad. The death rate in relation to weight increase is steeper for women and men younger than 50 years old and the mortality rate increases with duration, as would be expected.

It behooves all of us, starting as young as possible, to get our weight to normal and stay there. The costs of obesity to us individually and as a nation are just too high - in body aches, heartaches, and in billions upon billions of dollars!

We can do it. We have a way now. Medicine has provided the effective treatment and cure. The following chapter will provide you with additional medical insight from another pioneer in the medical treatment of obesity, Dr. Steven Lamm, author of <u>Thinner At Last.</u>

Patient's Personal Comments

"I've been overweight off and on all my life due to overeating and not enough exercise. I feel my diagnosis of diabetes was in a sense a blessing. Sounds crazy - but true. I've been a sugar addict and food addict for years and now after a failure or two, I'm back on track with my diet and exercise, losing weight and getting closer to my goal."

Notes:

Notes:

Chapter Ten

In this chapter, you will receive additional information and insight on many points I have shared with you in the preceding chapters. We are truly entering a new age with unprecedented potential for healthier men, women, and children.

Patient's Personal Comments

"This is the only diet that has really worked for me. My blood sugar count is down and I hope I can get off insulin. I'm proud of myself and Dr. Darland."

A Second Opinion

The importance of weight control is evident in its growing popularity as a subject for magazine covers and television documentaries. Unfortunately, "sensationalism sells," as media moguls say, and many features dealing with this very serious subject come down to nothing more than exploiting public concern with misleading headlines and sensational half-truths.

Mistakes in this vital health area can literally be fatal. Before beginning even a simple exercise program, you are cautioned by responsible trainers to consult with your physician and have a physical examination. Fad diets can threaten your health in addition to wasting your time and money.

It is my contention that weight control is basic to your health and, as such, is first and foremost a matter to discuss with your primary care doctor. It is my purpose in this book, as it is in Dr. Lamm's book *Thinner at Last*, to help both patients and physicians come to this understanding. Even though, since its publishing, Phen-fen itself has been discontinued because of possible fatal side effects, the principle of a pharmaceutical approach to the treatment of obesity - overweightness was established.

I have been privileged to visit with Dr. Lamm on occasion and had the pleasure of hearing him speak on "Advances in the Treatment of Obesity" at a seminar in my home state of Illinois.

At the seminar, Dr. Lamm emphasized that obesity is pathology, a disease, which is not the patients' fault even though they often are blamed for their condition. He outlined numerous medical and psychological consequences which no one would freely choose to suffer.

I was struck by his references to studies which highlight the social stigma of obesity in the minds of both those who are overweight and those who are not, studies which show: that the young college student would rather go out with a cocaine user or embezzler than date someone who is described as fat; that 80% of teenage girls have been on a diet to lose weight and that they have more fear of being fat than of nuclear war or the loss of a child; that people who have become thin would rather be deaf, blind, or lose a leg than to be fat again.

In short, the medical and social consequences of obesity are so severe they should suggest to us that some underlying condition or compulsion must be a major contributing factor.

Dr. Lamm cited advances in understanding made possible by the insight of Dr. Weintraub, who first articulated in scientific papers that obesity is a disease which is part medical-physiological and part medical-psychological, requiring use of proactive medications - Phentermine and Fenfluramine - to deal with both aspects of the disease. Of course, this combination is no longer available because of the dangerous side effects.

It was interesting for me to hear that Dr. Lamm's experience with Phen-Fen began in the same manner mine did. He said a patient brought him an article about "this great, new discovery" and urged him to research it and determine if it could help her. Like my patient, his had tried repeatedly to lose weight, but nothing had worked.

When Dr. Lamm determined the approach was sound, the patient began her treatment. She weighted 350 pounds at that time. She now weighs 160 pounds, close to her "thin weight," and has used her new-found energy to earn a Master's Degree in Exercise Physiology from Colombia University.

He cited experiences with other patients who had tried "every imaginable diet" without success - a predictable result in light of our new knowledge about the disease dimension of obesity. When he introduced the patients to the medical approach, their cravings disappeared and they ate differently. His experience paralleled mine in the familiar patient response, "I used to think of food 90%

of the time. Now I don't anymore with the medicine." Those of us who are free from food obsession may never be able to fully appreciate how freeing that release from preoccupation with food can be.

He also cited genetic predisposition causes. Examples included twins who were separated at birth and reunited at age 25. Though reared in totally different environments, both were driven by the same "genetic mapping" and both were grossly obese. He also cited studies of babies who suck three times harder than other babies in nursing and get 20% more milk. Such studies reveal the powerful genetic forces operating in obesity.

Dr. Lamm said will power and motivation can play a role in obesity, but those forces also may be genetically driven. He referred to Dr. Leibovich at the Rockefeller Institute in Manhattan, who has done research on the neuropeptides and other neuro-hormones that stimulate us to eat and tell us when to stop eating. If they are deficient, the normal response is absent and eating gets out of control.

He cited clinical experience results prior to the Phen-Fen breakthrough which showed that 95% of lost weight would be gained back. His description of the typical pattern before the new development was a four-month cycle of failure. In the first month, the doctor would give you a diet, a pep talk about changing your lifestyle, tell you to exercise, and have you come back. In the second month, you failed, so the doctor would send you to a nutritionist. In the third month, you failed with the nutritionist, so the doctor would send you to a psychiatrist. In the fourth month, you failed with the psychiatrist, too, so you and your doctor both threw up your hands in defeat and decided to forget the whole thing.

In that era, the medical profession was locked into the idea that weight loss was a matter of will. Most believed as U.S.A. Olympic Weightlifting coach and strong man Bob Hoffman stated in his book *How To Be Healthy,*

Happy, And Strong, "Ninety-eight percent of overweightness is due to gluttony, lack of character and will, and laziness."

Dr. Lamm pointed out how ignorant it is to blame overweight patients for their condition in light of genetic predisposition discoveries cited earlier and Dr. Weintraub's confirmation of the neuro-chemistry dimension of obesity in his double-blind, placebo controlled, randomized study. The obesity factors had been there, "right in front of our faces," he said. Both Phentermine and Fenfluramine had been on the market for 25 years treating entities separately, but it was not until Dr. Weintraub completed his research that we understood how to use them to heal patients suffering the affliction of obesity. Now for me, it's usually Prozac instead of Pondimin.

Now we are in a new era, Dr. Lamm said, similar to the advent of penicillin after Fleming. Before that antibiotic treatment, fifty percent of all pneumonia patients died. Before Dr. Weintraub, we had an even worse failure rate with obesity. Now, just as we can cure most pneumonia patients, we can cure patients of their obesity. This new approach recognizes that medicine may be a necessity, not an option in the treatment of this disease.

Dr. Lamm recommended that the conventional diet and exercise approach to obesity be tried first, though 95% of patients will fail with diet and exercise alone because of the way they have been "scripted" genetically. Still others will fail because of certain environmental triggers which are not yet completely understood. He said telling those patients to lose weight is like telling an asthmatic to stop wheezing, an alcoholic to stop drinking, or ordering someone's eyes to turn blue. It is much deeper than that, a biological matter.

He asked us to consider all the reasons people eat. We eat when we are hungry, of course, but also when we are agitated, bored, or in a crisis. We turn to food - particularly to the carbohydrates such as potatoes, bread, spaghetti - to reduce agitation in the brain. Others do not lock into carbohydrates. Instead they drink alcohol, take drugs, etc.

The diet and exercise approach cannot help with the agitation-generated eating response nor does the psychiatric approach. The problem is in the area of neuro-chemical stimulus, a medical problem. That is where the medication comes in. The full treatment is diet, exercise, behavior modification, and medication. Only a doctor can help with the medication, Dr. Lamm added, "That's why Richard Simmons wants to be a doctor. He knows where it is."

But he pointed out there are detractors for this approach, despite the great promise it has shown. Some critics say doctors are too quick to provide the medicine. First we are criticized for not providing it enough, now we are criticized for providing it too much. Others question the safety. The new medicine approach is really quite safe, he said, but it has to be monitored well. The treatment is imperfect and the medicines are imperfect, but they are all we have right now. Now we mostly use Phentermine, Meridia, Xenical and Prozac.

He described Phentermine as a stimulant and a distant relative of the amphetamine family and as non-addictive. "In twenty years of practice in New York City, I have not had one person come to my office wanting Phentermine. Actually, it's no more than a cup of coffee. There are no side effects, except maybe a little dry mouth or jitteriness that's usually gone in five days."

Of course, as of September 15, 1997 Fenfluramine (Pondimin and Redux) is no longer available; but they got the ball rolling, as I said before and we may get these medicines or others as good, in the future. Maybe a drug like Fenfluramine will be available again some day without the side effects. The major thing that Phen-Fen did was to show that medicine was very important in the treatment of obesity. PPH is associated with shortness of breath, leg edema or swelling, and hypertension, symptoms and signs which can lead to death. It occurs in only one to three people per million in the population. With Fenfluramine or Redux, it is supposedly eighteen to forty-five per million.

The physician and patient must decide the risk to benefit ratio for all medications. If you take aspirin, you can bleed to death; 1,000 do each year. If you take estrogen, you can have a stroke. All medicines have some risks.

Dr. Lamm said the length of treatment can vary from a short time to a lifetime, as with diabetes or hypertension, and reminded us that there may be many new regimens on the horizon, just as there will be new medicines, all tailored to the individual patient's needs.

He describes himself as being on a "mission" in this work. His enthusiasm is almost overwhelming as he describes our new beginning in the treatment of obesity. We are on what he calls the "frontier" right now. We are the "pathfinders," the "forgers," and he communicates a sense of urgency because obesity is the second most common cause of preventable death in this country at least 300,000 death per year. First is lung cancer from smoking. Obesity is rapidly overcoming it for the first place position. The approach must be clinical, he cautions, but we have to help our people, and we shall. We are the innovators!

In the next chapter, I will provide you with a summary overview of where we are and where we are going.

Notes:

Notes:

Patient's Personal Comments

"I feel great from morning till night. I didn't know it could be so easy. I've struggled for years. I wish everyone who has a weight problem would hear about your program."

"I have felt 'fat' from as far back as I can remember. It never stops. I had a petite older sister who made me look even heavier. I have been on every diet, from Weight Watchers to Slender Center to TOPS. I've tried them all and put on more weight after each attempt. My reckoning was more like a last ditch effort. I came to Dr. Darland and he was so encouraging. I felt better immediately. The program is the greatest, you're up, your confidence soars. I lost 20 pounds in 26 days and lost 23 inches. I know I can make it."

Chapter Eleven

In this chapter, you will find an overview of points we have covered, a capsule version for quick review when you need a little boost to help you stay the course and reach your goal. All of us need reminders and encouragement to persevere. Turn to this chapter when you need a quick refresher course.

Patient's Personal Comments

"This program has been a lifesaver for me physically and emotionally also, and I like to hear people say, 'My God you look good.' So thank you again for this program and all the encouragement."

The Summing Up

"I am trying to lose weight and I can't do it on my own."

Until recently, that familiar refrain was a call for help no one could fully answer. It was ultimately an expression of frustration and admission of defeat for many.

Now those words are nothing more than a candid assessment of reality and a request for help modern medicine finally can deliver in your primary care doctor's office.

Before moving on to answer frequently asked questions about this new, holistic approach to health through weight control, I want to review some of the key elements we have covered. Repetition is a great teacher -and "doctor" does mean "teacher," of course. A summary chapter also provides you with a fast recap and guide for future reference.

In these pages, you have learned why past weight control efforts have failed and what new help is available. You have learned that weight problems have multiple, complex causes, all of which must be addressed to bring about a lifetime cure.

In the chapter "Helpless and Hopeless? Not Any More," you learned about my patients who are able to overcome lifelong weight control problems with the modern, holistic approach I advocate. They are able to attain and maintain normal, fit healthy weight and find new enjoyment in life - once and for all! And you learned that the same help which has changed their lives is calorie restriction, but I believe virtually everyone knows that. Certainly anyone interested in this topic does. It is not knowing *what to do* that is the problem, however. Applying it, getting there, and staying there, *that is* the hard part. Proper diet fosters wellness, but if dieting alone were sufficient to solve the weight control problems we face, there would be far fewer books about dieting and far more normal weight, healthy, fit trim people.

We dealt with another vital element in the chapter "Exercise - Who Needs It? We All

Do.

Exercise saves us from many unnecessary afflictions which sideline and even kill the sedentary. You learned that all of us need to exercise - aerobically and isotonically - to achieve and maintain freedom from obesity. You learned that getting the exercise you need is simple and inexpensive. I urged you to take advantage of what are called environmental exercise opportunities - climbing steps instead of riding on escalators and elevators, carrying grocery bags to the car instead of wheeling them in a cart, for example. And I advised you to get three days of isotonics and three days of aerobics each week.

In the "Behavior Modification" chapter, you learned that you must change some of your habits so you do more of what helps you and less or none of what hurts you. I outlined and elaborated on what I call the "four pillars" which underlie successful weight control programs. First, you must be motivated, that is, you must be *ready*, resolved, determined, and committed. Second, you must follow a *diet.* Third, you must eat foods *low in fat.* Fourth, you must *exercise.* As you read in this chapter and have noted in my patients' comments throughout the book, the medication makes it easier, but you must make the changes which will guarantee your success. The medication helps you modify your behavior and your behavior modification in turn helps the medication do its work. Together they help you reach your goal of fit and healthy living. I also need to add that we have very good surgery available for the severely recalcitrant obese - namely the Roux-en-Y. Twenty-six of my patients have undergone this procedure.

Just when you realized you finally had the solution to weight management and thought you had everything under control, you learned about another obstacle to your success in the chapter on "The Saboteurs." They are people who consciously or unconsciously try to undermine you. Often they are our loved ones and people you see every day. Some saboteurs are well intentioned but misguided. Others are threatened by your success and become the victims of their own basic and strong psychological defense mechanisms. In this chapter, I warned you to be aware of the destructive dynamics at work and to fortify yourself against the saboteurs' tricks and temptations. Be charitable and understanding and forgiving, but do not let them derail you. Remember, their reactions are their problems, not yours. You know weight loss and fitness are right for you, good for you, healthy for you, so be confident and stay on course.

A powerful help for staying on course is a healthy personal philosophy, which you read about in Chapter 8, "Philosophy: Who Needs It? We All Do." You learned that your personal philosophy, your "Weltanschauung" or worldview, can provide you with added power to drive the task, make you more forceful, more persistent, and more likely to succeed. Having your own philosophy enables you to have a clear picture of who you are and what you are and what your purpose in life is. It helps you understand yourself better, know what is best for you, and do what is best. It gives you the strength to avoid and resist those who would lure you off course with distractions and detractions.

"The Medical Hazards Of Obesity Or 'How Bad Is It Doctor?'" provided you with a catalog of afflictions and complications of obesity. The bad news is that the list of harmful effects in the chapter is not complete and probably never could be. The list grows with research. The good news is that your primary care doctor now has an effective treatment and cure for obesity which can free you from those harmful effects.

In Chapter 10, "A Second Opinion," I served in the manner of newspaper reporter to provide you with additional information and insight with Information learned from Dr. Stephen Lamm, author of Thinner At Last, in private practice, and Clinic Assistant Professor of Medicine at New York University, N.Y.

Being fit and trim really boils down to using common sense. Why be miserable when you can be happy? Why be sick when you can be well? Why shop for clothes to cover up your bulges when you can shop for clothes you really would like to wear?

Treating and curing obesity also boil down to using common sense now. When your car does not run properly, you take it to a mechanic. When your appliances fail, you call a repair service. Certainly your body deserves at least as much consideration and care as cars and appliances receive. The repair and care your overweight body needs is available at your primary care doctor's office.

Now that you have an overview of this medical breakthrough, a new understanding of how it works and what it can do for you, turn to the next chapter for answers to frequently asked questions about this new and exciting development.

Notes:

Notes:

Patient's Personal Comments

"Before meeting Dr. Darland I always believed overweight people (including myself) just 'ate too much,' but now I believe it is a disease that can be treated with medication. By treating this disease I am warding off many other overweight-related diseases."

"Seven months ago I tried to turn over in bed to answer the ringing telephone. When I couldn't turn my self over, at the age of 32 and approximately 12 years of being overweight, I decided to call for help! I fortunately knew where the 'help' came from. I had been told by a friend, of a kind and wise doctor whose name was Darland. I finally reached the telephone, not in time to answer it, but in time to re-shape and re-claim my life! I called Dr. Darland that day and made the most important appointment of my life! Seven months later and 64 pounds later, I have and will continue to re-claim my life, re-shape my destiny and carve a new future for myself!"

Chapter Twelve

In this chapter, you will learn still more about the rapidly developing and expanding world of wellness through weight control. I will answer questions frequently raised by both patients and doctors who are new to this medical breakthrough. Some questions will deal with recently released medicines and other approaches.

Patient's Personal Comments

"Since I started this diet, I have more energy and I actually enjoy exercising. When I go to the store I read labels now; before I didn't. I've learned how to cook and eat healthy. I don't have to listen to people tell me how to eat and what because I learned this from you. God Bless you for the wonderful work you are doing. Thank you for your support."

"Dr. Darland, we have had a 30 year relationship. You have seen me thin and you have seen me at my highest weight of 263 pounds. I always vowed to myself I would never get too fat as my mom was. As you and I both know, I became very unhealthy with the excess weight. I decided to try once again to lose weight. This program has been a lifesaver for me, both emotionally and physically. My daughter and I are both on the plan and are both succeeding in our joint venture to become as healthy as we can. When we need encouragement we talk and find a mutual

agreed upon way to exercise or maybe a little reminder of how much help we truly get from our medication and encouragement from you! Thanks again."

Questions and Answers

Q. Where can I go to get into a medical weight loss program?

A. Call your own Doctor, your local medical society, the ASBP (American Society of Bariatric Physicians), the AOA (American Obesity Association), the North American Association for the Study of Obesity (NAASO) or ask a friend who has been through it.

Q. Does Meridia work?

A. We had a study of 384 patients - citing this was to be the replacement for Phen-Fen. We may have a lot fewer patients using this medicine now. The jury is still out, but it has been out on the market since February 14, 1998. It may go up in dose, and other changes are in the works for Meridia. The "Storm" trial reported at Geensboro, N.C. in August, 2000 showed 15% weight lose in 2 years.

Q. Can you safely use Phen/Xen together?

A. I use it. We explain all factors in detail and

have the patient sign a "disclaimer". This is so patients realize it hasn't been studied or published this way so far. It is very unlikely it can cause harm. Only 1% of Xenical is absorbed in the blood stream. To date, after 2 years use of Phen/Xen and over 2,000 patients, we have not had <u>one</u> serious side effect with their associated use.

Q. Will Phen/Fen ever come back?

A. I don't think so. There were statistically significant side-effects and fatalities as a result of its use. Albeit, if only in a very small incidence this was true. There were cardiac valve problems (Heidi Connally, Mayo Clinic Cardiologist July 7, 1997); and an increase of Primary Pulmonary Hypertension (actually "acquired") allegedly and convinsingly stated by the work of Stuart Rich, M.D. of the University of Illinois, Chicago, and Presby terian, St. Lukes Hospital, Chicago. On the other hand A research paper by Andrew Burger, et. al., of Boston, Massachusetts, with 224 patients on Phen/Fen over a three year period, 1994 - 1997, with "echo's" before and "echo's" after, showed no difference in valve regurgitation, compared to the Framingham Heart study for age matched patients (American Journal of Cardiology, Oct. 1999).

I had 3,420 patients on Phen/Fen from 1992 through September 15, 1997. In a specific study group of 1647, 508 of them got their body weight to absolutely "normal." Twenty-eight patients lost over 100 pounds or more, nearly a one-third success rate. As cited by the F.D.A. The combination is prohibited. We know this disease is risky and sometimes the treatment is risky like in surgery. A doctor would not knowingly risk a fatality when there is a safer method.

Q. What about the "relapse" after the weight is off and you've gone through the course of medication?

A. Relapse with obesity-overweightness should be treated the same way as with any chronic disease such as Diabetes, Hypertension, Asthma. The doctor and patient have to get onto the regimen again: diet, exercise, good lifestyle adherence, and medicine - maybe all for a lifetime.

Q. How about treating patients with minimal overweightness?

A. Generally I think all overweightness unhinges optimal health and fitness. If medicine is needed, I personally feel it is justified. Even 15% overweightness may cause artery plaquing.

Q. What's the future for the treatment of obesity?

A. 1)   There will be more understanding with the realization that in 95% of the patients this is a genetically predisposed problem;

2)   This is a problem that is chronic and recurrent like asthma, hypertension and diabetes problems;

3)   Life style is very important, like getting into an aerobic-isotonic exercise program, watching the fats, and not

overeating for pleasure or as a stress reliever; and lastly,

4) Medicine is O.K. There will be newer and better pharmaceuticals in the future, but we have good medicines now. Patients and Doctors have to embrace this approach which may be life saving and absolutely necessary.

Q. What is the Roux-en-Y surgical procedure?

A. This is a surgical approach for the treatment of stubborn obesity that is killing the patient. It's a one-and-a-half hour procedure that cuts the stomach into a 1- 2 ounce pouch and sews the edges up away from each other, Half way down of the ten feet of the small intestines it is cut in two. The bottom half is hauled up and attached to the small pouch of the stomach entered into the esophagus (food tube). There is absolutely no food absorption in the front part of the small intestine, the cut end of which is connected to the lower part of the small intestine. This procedure has been done on 26 of my patients so far. It does not have the bad effects of the old procedure like "dumping", diarrhea and electrolyte imbalance. You have to be over 100 pounds overweight or 80 pounds overweight with morbidities (sequelae of severe obesity). I am very thrilled about this necessary severe approach to obesity treatment. It has been life saving to thousands of patients who have no other successful way so far.

Notes:

Notes:

Patient's Personal Comments

"I was a track 'star' in school, in Pom-poms, and was 110- 115 pounds. I was lean and mean. After high school I went to college and was no longer as active, and one month ago I weighed 148 pounds. I can't even begin to tell you how difficult it was to look at myself I cried, put myself down and was terribly depressed. Here I was, 21 years old with lots of stretch marks and it wasn't from having children. Then I discovered Dr. Darland and his program. Not only am I not hungry all the time, but I eat much smaller portions. I am so grateful to Dr. Darland. He really helps people who are overweight. I'm much more positive about myself and everything around me. The cold, hard, unyielding chains of food are coming off? Thanks so much!"

Harry W. Darland M.D.

2350 N Rockton Av.

Suite 209

Rockford, IL 61103

815 962 8150; FAX 815 962 8153

Addenda

Karen and I attended a meeting of the Roche Pharmaceutical Company on an "update on Meridia" the drug that was launched Valentines Day 1998. It has a two year 8 .mouth staying power now with an impressive impact on the medical treatment of obesity and overweightness. There were some 115 "Leaders in the treatment of obesity" invited with a seminar and review status presented by some of the "gurus" in the field of Bariatrics present. Karen and I were honored as the only private practicing Family Practitioners invited from the State of Lincoln, with a population of 13.5 million Americans, 54% of whom are overweight.

We learned a lot; especially that obesity and overweightness are indeed a medical "problem" - if you don't want to say "disease". Just as hypertension, diabetes and asthma are a medical "problem" with just as much complexity and dire consequences that they are a disease, obesity should be treated as such. Many of medical practitioners won't accept obesity - overweightness as a medical "disease". Many of my colleagues won't accept this entity into their medical purview of necessary medical treatment entities. They won't accept obesity as a medical disease - or even a medical problem. To them it belongs in the area of a psychosocial cultural problem - out of their realm as medical concern.

Many medical practitioners will accept the consequences of obesity - overweightness as a medical problem - disease, however. I talked with Dr. Arthur Frank, head of the prestigious obesity nutrition department at

George Washington University in Washington D.C., at this meeting; and Karen and I had dinner with him last March at the Wyeth - Ayrest fat blocker drug Xenical (Orlistat) conference. Dr. Frank has made great headway at the nutritional obesity treatment center at Georgetown University in Washington D.C. He is an impressive physician in many ways with the charisma endearing of a true leader in this field. He was quoted some years back in the AMA medical tribune weekly newspaper as saying "Obesity is the harbinger of many diseases that can cause terrible afflictions to the human body." Some years back I had read the same quote of a physician from the island of Cos in Greece. He said, "Obesity is the harbinger of many disease that can cause terrible afflictions to the human body". All physicians revere this Greek physician and even follow his Oath like Dr. Frank and I do. That brilliant prescient Physician's name was "Hippocrates," I have, his bust in my library; and his picture in the hallway of my office.

All of us that attended those Atlanta and

Greensboro meetings accept obesity overweightness as a disease. The next step then is to analyze its causes, character, and treatment regimens. All physicians should do this; and, all related "paramedicals" and persons in positions of responsibility, that could result in treating obesity, should be treating this problem as a disease associated with its illnesses.

It is my basic opinion trained as a Zoologist, and physician, with thirty-five years experience trying my hardest to treat the recalcitrant obesity - overweight patient that it is a genetic predisposition to be overweight in over 95% of the incidences. It is not our fault. It is the natural result of our mechanisms - mostly residing in our genes, and imbedded in our brains. Of course we have the substrate of the modern society of humans that lends to little exercise, too much food to eat (for the most "civilized" of nations) especially fatty foods.

The treatment then for the recalcitrant overweight patient is to teach the brain not be hungry (like with an adrenergic agent like phentermine); and to teach the brain not to have this appetite when we are not hungry with the serotonergic agents, like Prozac. In many cases pharmaceutical and other behavioral techniques are not adequate to treat obesity. That is where bariatric surgery comes in: presently the Roux-en-y gastric exclusion procedure. Thousands of patients have been "cured" of their obesity by this heroic means, Heroic efforts continue to be positioned, and more will come. These coupled with lifestyle changes (behavioral modifications) and "rule setting " in early teaching will accomplished the goal of "normal weight... and conquer the disease and all its terrible sequalae; immediately, financially, and psychologically, with all it's poignant heartbreaks

This was the conclusion of the Greensboro, Meridia meeting. There were "standouts" in the presenters of the different aspects of obesity concerns. One was Dr. John Fernstrom from the University of Pittsburgh Medical School. He is a neuro-biochemist. He has written over 200 papers on this subject. His area of interest on study is where our research on development of new drugs will come to combat this disease. At a previous meeting in New York he stated that our brains, and we humans are very complex. What works for one in this disease doesn't work for another. He said that with about 100 billion brain cells (the same as the estimated galaxies in our universe); and with their 100 trillion connections we have quite a task in this research, development and treatment of overweightness - obesity. He said its like going through a jungle with a machete trying to find the way. Nevertheless, he is one of the undaunted heroes in this search for help in this disease.

Ann Wolf was another standout in this meeting. She has a consulting firm and is president of "Ann Wolf Associates" that offers advise on management on the tremendous loss in dollars to 1000's of companies and corporations across our nation. She spoke to us about how obesity in itself causes such serious economic losses related to employment. She cited that the direct health care costs of obesity only to industry and business is 51.6 billion dollars per year. Absenteeism; less efficiency, psychological detriment, are just some of the major causes of obesity related costs to our working society.

One study by Kaiser Permanente of Colorado cited by Ann Wolf showed patients with BMI's of 30 -35 (moderately obese) had a 25% increase of health care costs over the normal weight individual. If the BMI was over 37 (severely obese) the cost was 44% over the normal weight individual.

Also all studies show that as BMI increase, lifetime health care costs increase in an upsurging linear fashion Wolf says.

Further statistics of the Greensboro Ann Wolf seminar were these: total costs of obesity to the U.S. of obesity direct and indirect were 99.2 billion dollars,, Obesity per se. 65 billion dollars. Even a modest overweightness has health costs such as hyperlipidemia (fat in the blood) and increased artery plaquing. Coronary plaquing causes 1/3 of all deaths in the USA 1.1 million per year; one third of whom don't even make it to the hospital. Disability days in one study cited by Wolf were 5.9% and 4.7% for normal males and females respectfully; and 9.8 and 12.6% for the obese males and females respectfully a two time increase in males, obese; and three times for females, obese. The morbid statistics went on and on for what she called the deadly "6" of obesity in regards to the overall debilities death, disease, disorganization, duty, dissatisfaction and destitution.

Ann Wolf expressed hopefully that employers and insurance companies would be taking a more and more active role in stemming this tide of obesity tragedies. She also noted that the Surgeon General announced he will be taking a very proactive role in leadership in fighting the Fat of the Land, (title of a very insightful and informative book on Obesity in America written by Michael Fumento, 1997 Viking Press!)

I would like to end this book on some antidotes; some stories about some of my heroic patients and their doctors.

The first story is about Patty. Patricia Snider has two children, Andrew 10, and Adam, 6. Patty's journey to normal weight and fitness, started about when we, barbell blokes noticed Patty walking the YMCA track - and walking and walking. The track is just next door to our free weights and machine gym at the "Y" where the two Mike's Willie and I and others workout. It's only separated from us by glass, and I have to say Patty was very attractive then, even at her 196 pounds start.

I interviewed Patty for this section and she said she eventually walked 2 laps and ran I lap and so on and so on many days a week. Patty said she started the weights and machines about 8 months into it. A friend of Patty's and mine, Dan Johnson, a SCUBA instructor and travel trip director for SCUBA experiences in the waters all around the world extolled the virtues of weight training as well as aerobics. Dan realizes the great importance of these two aspects of fitness in his sport and recreation; so, he was eager to start Patty out. She was an eager and apt student, and she quickly became a regular strength trainer as well as a runner. Patty told me she does about one hour of aerobics and isotonics (strength training). Patty's routine. is to run 2 - 3 miles on the bike path next to the river starting at our Rockford YMCA (the greatest "Y" in the world)- out and back - a great arrangement-safe and efficient.

One day she does upper body isotonics like arm curls and presses etc.; and the next day she does the lower body, like leg presses and squats. She said she "stumbled around" at first; but now she's in a very good and likeably fun routine that exercises her whole body in strength and flexibility and aerobic endurance. She says she mixes it up, changes routines to make it interesting and fun, and to challenge all the muscle groups.

I asked her about her diet, and she said it's a "well - balanced diet that has proper nutrition". She takes no vitamins and no supplements. She imparted with a smile that she has to watch it at times because she took her children to our local pumpkin patch, apple orchard place at "Edwards Apple Orchard" near Rockford, and she downed 4 warm cinnamon donuts with apple cider before you could say Jack Spratt! She said, "Once people are heavy they will always have a fear they will eat too much and be fat." At times she eats as much as her 240-pound muscled construction worker boyfriend; so, she is "always on guard to keep the balance."

"I know I'm much healthier now," Patty said;" and I can do so much more and have fun at it like playing a good game of volleyball with my friends - and I'm proud of how I look now." "But Dr, Darland," she said with a sad expression; I've got this image of myself in my mind of being a self conscious, fat girl. I know I'm not now - maybe it'll go away some day."

I'm so proud of Patty. Patty did this all on her own with determination, self-motivation. Of course she had encouragement from friends-like Dan. I'm convinced Patty has a good outlook for sustained normal weight, and fitness. Not that she doesn't have to work at it, and be ever vigilant to the rules of good health and fitness; but she will make it. Now at 5'6" and 127 pounds (from 196#, a 49 pound loss!) her medium frame is adorned with beauty, and fitness. Her attitude and personality is sparkling. In short, Patty is the totally wonderful type of person that we all admire; and she did it herself.

Elizabeth is another story, She came to me on April 3rd of 1997 to start the Phen - Fen diet because "I can't do it myself even though I've tried and tied, and I've struggled and struggled." There is nothing wrong with Elizabeth. She is normal. But Elizabeth was overweight and couldn't get it off She knew that to be overweight and to lose it to normal weight "helps everything" as she interrupted me in my presentation when she came back as a "restart" last Thursday, October 26, 2000.

On April 3rd 1997 she started the Phen - Fen program and lost 14 pounds the first month and 12 pounds the second month. Her start weight was 175 pounds at 5'6" tall. She listed her ideal body weight then at 125lb.

She has kept most of it off - not quite to goal - then she started to gain again on her restart. Her weight was 163 pounds and she listed her IBW at 140 pounds. She couldn't control it; so, on 10/27/00 she came back for pharmaceutical help and any other advice that might help. I placed her on the Phen - Xen program and advised her to eat a lower caloric well balanced diet, follow the rules, and come back 10 pounds less in 1 month. I know she will. She will see Karen, my wife, manager and medical assistant until she reaches goal. Then she will come back as needed until she stays at goal for 2 years. She's enthusiastic, and so are Karen and I. She is going to make it this time.

She is an example of a line of survivors. There is overweightness in her family just as there was in her caveman ancestry who packed on the weight to survive the famine, especially around fall when animals and tubers would be scarce, during the winter. "Mother Nature" genetically drives us to eat through our hunger and appetite brain - body mechanism. Its not being weak – willed or character - flawed, it's being a human. We have to sometimes trick Mother Nature into our not feeling hungry, and not having a ravenous appetite through pharmaceuticals like Phen - Xen or Meridia, or Xenical alone or with an SSRI and an adrenergic drug like Dr. Michael Anchors did. As I cited earlier, he reported this in his book <u>Safer than Phen -Fen</u>, He explained the great results he got with Phentermine (Adipex) and Fluoxetine (Prozac). He called this combination "Phen - Pro" (August, 1997).

This book came out about a month after Dr. Heidi Conally of Mayo Clinic announced her findings about the controversial heart valve and blood pressure problems that may have occurred with the use of Phen - Fen - July 7, 1997, at a world - wide announcement. There were probably 60 million Phen - Fen users at that time in an attempt to stem this disease - causing the society-related scourge called obesity overweightness.

Elizabeth hasn't far to go. We will nip the problem in the bud, and it will be gone for this very matter of fact, lovely patient of ours.

Pat Boyer is another story. She has lost 96 pounds starting with Phen - Fen – ending with close to normal weight. Of course she included exercise, and it has been an inseparable adjunct to her problem solving of her obesity. She told me, "Dr. Darland, tell them you can't make it without exercise coming into play eventually."

After the corporation, "Home Health Products" pulled Fen (Pondimin and Redux) from the market at the urging of the FDA; Pat needed to find a way to continue the weight loss and keep it off. She has done it, with the trial and error and finally a formula that fits her; Phentermine, (hunger suppressant), Xenical (the fat blocker); and Wellbutrin SR (Bupropion hydrochloride, the Adrenergic, Serotonergic, and Dopaminergic" - "pot pourri" drug combo). We might call her pharmaceutical anorexiant, Dopaminergic lipid blocker combination the Well/Phen/Xen program. Of course, she is in the behavioral modification mode, as well as being an avid and very admirable exerciser. Pat B looks great, feels great, is much healthier; but she is still struggling hard to maintain.

Lastly there are three stories that involve the use of another method to solve stubborn obesity problems. This is called bariatric surgery, the Roux-en-Y gastric exclusion procedure. There is a long history of valiant attempts to cure obesity with surgery. These were mainly the Jejunal by - pass, and gastric stapling surgeries. There were problems that made these two surgeries undesirable. Firstly, the Jejunal by - pass procedure caused cramping and diarrhea; as well as electrolyte imbalance, and essential nutrient, and vitamin malabsorption. The stapling procedure essentially just broke down and returned the stomach as before.

Now we have a way surgically that is safe, effective with definite compliance by the nature of the gastric exclusion. There is only a

1-2 oz. Reservoir of stomach left after the surgical reduction. One half of the small intestine of the 10 feet is by - passed so there is further definite compliance to lower caloric absorption.

Mike was also a Phen/Fen patient, and he was one of my 28 patients who lost over 100 pounds on the Phen/Fen program. Prior to that weight loss, he was miserable. He had Sleep Apnea Syndrome requiring a mask for forced breathing at night - the so called C - Pap mask. His knees hurt from obesity associated with degenerative arthritis; and he was quite depressed - like about 20% of patients are that are more than 40% overweight.

All this changed when he lost the 112 pounds on Phen/Fen. He got rid of the Sleep Apnea and his night C - Pap masks. His knees have felt better; psychologically his depression lifted and he generally felt great. He was on a maintenance program when Pondimin and Redux were pulled from the market - the two forms of Fenfluramine.

As you might expect, Mike was a so called "non- - responder" to all the other means for weight loss pharmaceutically, and behaviorly. At my urging, he decided to visit the Northwest Community Bariatric Center Hospital in Belvedere, Illinois. This is one of the centers in the the Mid - West that is part of a corporation whose main objective is to help patients by surgery who have severe obesity that has not responded to treatment by all other means. Dr. Eric Schlesinger and Dr. Roy Berkowitz are the two main surgeons in that hospital in Belvidere. They are assisted by Dr. Kestas Simkus, a surgeon of some 20 years experience, mostly in Lithuania.

Mike visited the hospital, and met with the very efficient team of insurance experts, nurses, administrators and Dr. Berkowitz. He met the criteria; he had gained back nearly all the weight he lost! Criteria one is over 100 pounds over weight, criteria two is at least 80 pounds overweight with two or more morbidities - like sleep apnea syndrome, and degenerative knee arthritis. Mike is quite a guy.

In the whole difficult procedure of getting his weight to normal, he developed a malignant brain tumor that was treated and cured. Then he had his Roux-en-Y gastric exclusion procedure. He has lost 73 pounds so far from his operation date of July 24, 2000. I believe Mike is cured of obesity now and all its terrible sequelae. Thanks to the revolutionary new surgery and its consistently good results. I just interviewed Mike yesterday. We are both pleased with Drs. Schlesingers & Berkowitz's work.

I'll tell you more about the procedure when I tell you about my last patient to have it performed, Benedetta Bucemi. Betty wanted me to be there with her; so, I scrubbed in with Dr. David Schlesinger, and Dr. Kestas Simkus; his assistant; and viewed the procedure first hand.

I visited Betty first in the pre - op holding room where she received her preparation for surgery, She smiled at me when I offered my support and reassurance; and thanked me for being there with her and her family. I looked for her Mom, Gina and Grandmother, Maria next who were up in the surgical waiting room and visited with them. This hospital is devoted totally to the Bariatric Roux - en - Y gastric exclusion surgery. The doctors, Schlesinger and Berkowitz, perform two surgeries in the AM and two in the PM five days a week. Their waiting list is three months.

I scrubbed in with Dr. Eric Schlesinger for Betty's surgery, the first case in the afternoon of 9/7/00. We started at 1:55 PM and ended at 4:00 PM (skin to skin).

Eric related to me that there has been work in trying to do the procedure by laparoscopy - like a "lap - Choly" (scope - choycystectomy - gall bladder); but- it was fraught with problems of "exposure" requirements, and loosening of anatomical structure etc. that has to be done with a full view. The lap-Roux-en-Y, he said, may take as long as 4-5 hours. This like any other medical procedure or operations has to meet "standards of care," and these doctors are very attuned to these excellent standards. Their hospital is very professional, and well organized. The facility is meticulously clean, and their procedures and equipment are of very high standards. Interestingly, Dr. Schlesinger's wife is a lawyer, Joanne Schlesinger - actually a malpractice lawyer. Eric is very aware of good standards of care, and patient protection.

I stood shoulder to shoulder with Eric across from his assistant Dr. Sinkas. I was impressed by the deftness of their surgical skill, as well as, the way they approached and solved problems along the way. It was pure artistry, like listening to Mozart or Beethoven. We talked after Eric dictated in fine detail his transcript of his every move during the surgery.

The surgeons there use the Rockford Anesthesia group, headed by the very progressive and innovative anesthesiologist, Dr. Steve Minore of Rockford. Norbert Duttlinger, one of their 38 anesthesiologists, was Bettys' anesthesiologist. He stayed there monitoring her anesthesia and body condition every second. He used a balanced anesthesia of Versed, Fentanyl, and measured halogen products; measured to keep Betty safely asleep and pain free. One problem in her surgery was a suspension ligament of the liver that was getting in the way of the procedure. Dr. Schlesinger skillfully lyzed it free by his cautery wand.

The proximal segment of the "Y" (front half of the about 10 feet of small intestine) was 150 centimeters. The distal segment (bottom half) was 200 cm. He also noted some fatty infiltration of the viscera (fatty cells encroachment of the vital organs). That will go away when Betty is cured of obesity. He noted there was some fore-shortening of the omentum (fat apron of the abdomen over the intestines and organs) which made the procedure a little more difficult.

Eric used a "GI 100 stapler" to quickly cut and staple the edges of the stomach and intestine together when the machine fired. He used 2[0] mattress sutures of silk. There were other esoteric moves involving gastric tubes, bougies, and patches.

Eric irrigated the operating field copiously with cleansing fluid and closed with 3[0] nylon. The patient tolerated the procedure well.

Dr. Schlesinger noted that the 200-cm distal loop of small intestine was maintained to prevent diarrhea - a problem of earlier procedures. Eric related he has done over 700 Roux - en - Y's and the demand is increasing.

I interviewed Dr. Roy Berkowitz after Eric and I had finished Betty's procedure. Dr. Berkowitz also had an extremely interesting and thorough background of surgical training, and was obviously very enthusiastic about the great life-saving results they were getting. Roy said he especially liked the 1-year follow up visit when the patient's quality of life and outlook is so drastically changed.

Interestingly, he had just seen Lavella Friley, a long time patient of mine. I delivered her 8 year old Seddrick. She started at 426 pounds and is now at 271 pounds.

Lavella is beautiful in every way.

He said, "the GERD is gone, they no longer wake up 50 or more times at night with their sleep apnea syndrome. Their low back pain is now not a constant misery but is manageable in most cases. Their diabeties and hypertension is gone. All of their morbidities are gone; and it is especially good for their attitude, and their frame of mind generally is so beautifully changed. They are the most grateful patients I have ever dealt with - and this makes me feel great; in the realization that I was a large part of the difference. Mostly that I'm extending and saving their life."

Dr. Berkowitz and Schlesinger are both very modest and humble men; but their accomplishments are momentous, and beautifully poignant in every detail of these individual patient's life, function, and new feeling of self worth. Dr. Berkowitz sadly related the sorrowful discrimination the obese patients painfully and silently endure from others' treatment of them. He says that the "psychological morbidity" is heart rendering to him. He says it is pitiful the apologies the obese go through. They often become so ashamed of themselves because of the constant battering that society gives them like it was their fault.

He related that times are changing now with more awareness of the genetic and societal cause of obesity; and that we are all more understanding and cooperative now in this very important effort we are making to conquer this scourge called obesity-overweightness. I feel as these heroic doctors do, in their extreme measure of treatment, that we can conquer this disease, and we can cure it.

There are many notable leaders in this field of the treatment of obesity that of course I didn't mention. This work is just a part of theirs. I'm trying to do my part as a primary doctor who sees all types of patients, fifty percent of whom are overweight.

This is one of my areas of special interest in medicine. Just one area that needs continuing attention and hard work. I think patients can be "cured" of overweight and obesity. I don't think we should stop short of what is normal. I know it's hard but we should try. There was One who said "be you therefore perfect even which my Father in Heaven is perfect. " It's our destiny to try. We should keep trying! We can do it! - all together.

Notes: